SELF-PUBLISHING SECRETS

How To Self-Publish A Nonfiction Book On Amazon, Create The Manuscript, Get More Reviews, Sell More Books, Create A+ Content, and Much, Much, More

KEITH EVERETT

DISCLAIMER

The content contained within this book may not be reproduced, duplicated or transmitted without direct written permission from the author or the publisher.

Under no circumstances will any blame or legal responsibility be held against the publisher, or author, for any damages, reparation, or monetary loss due to the information contained within this book. Either directly or indirectly. You are responsible for your own choices, actions, and results.

Legal Notice:

This book is copyright protected. This book is only for personal use. You cannot amend, distribute, sell, use, quote or paraphrase any part, or the content within this book, without the consent of the author or publisher.

Disclaimer Notice:

Please note the information contained within this document is for educational and entertainment purposes only. All effort has been executed to present accurate, up to date, and reliable, complete information. No warranties of any kind are declared or implied. Readers acknowledge that the author is not engaging in the rendering of legal, financial, medical or professional advice. The content within this book has been derived from various sources. Please consult a licensed professional before attempting any techniques outlined in this book.

By reading this document, the reader agrees that under no circumstances is the author responsible for any losses, direct or indirect, which are incurred as a result of the use of the information contained within this document, including, but not limited to, — errors, omissions, or inaccuracies.

KDP, Kindle, Kindle Unlimited and Kindle Select are all registered trademarks of the Amazon Corporation.

FTC Notice: Some links in this book contain affiliate links whereby I will receive a small commission.

Copyright Keith Everett 2022 - All rights reserved.

ISBN-979-8428518580

CONTENTS

Introduction	vii
1. Scratch That Niche	1
2. The Magic Of Keywords	10
3. Creating That Amazing Manuscript	17
4. Hire A Ghostwriter Or Do It Yourself?	30
5. Should I Use A Pen Name Or Real Name?	35
6. Publishing Your Book On KDP	40
7. Finding The Right Categories For Your Book	53
8. Book Covers - DO It Yourself Or Pay Someone Else?	57
9. Getting Reviews	61
10. How To Sell More Books	72
11. Using Amazon Marketing Tools	78
12. Audible - Turning Sounds Into Profit	88
13. Setting Your Price and Getting Paid	97
14. A Word About Copyright	105
15. The Big Sell-Off	109
Conclusion	113
A Final Note From Keith	117
Resources	119

INTRODUCTION

Have you been thinking about dipping your toes into the self-publishing business, only to get cold feet when you find out how confusing it is?

Or did you wake up one day thinking, "I've got this," and start thumping away on your keyboard without a clue about how long it takes to write a book, what's involved, or how to publish it?

I hear you. Been there, done that. My first book, "Money Mind Crush", took me over a year to write. I had no experience whatsoever with writing, publishing, or any of that stuff. I just decided to make the move into self-publishing as a business, and I had to start somewhere.

Truthfully, I was all over the place. At first I found myself writing chapters out of sync, although it made sense to me, I think I would have confused my readers if I had published there and then.

I decided to buy a course.

I paid nearly $1000 to join a self-publishing course. After some trial and error, not to mention a lot of watching videos and experimentation, I finally began to see the light at the end of the tunnel.

I think that must have been the best $1000 I had ever spent.

Now, 2 years down the line and with 10 books under my belt, (some were written under a pen name) I can honestly say this really is the best business I've ever been in, and I've been in a lot. If you are keen to create a second income or even make a full-time living by self-publishing, there has never been a better time than now to get into it.

People love books. They always will, whether that is a paperback or an eBook or even an audiobook, the thirst for knowledge will never die.

In this book, I'm going to share everything I've learned about the self-publishing business with you. I know it can seem a bit intimidating at first, which is why I've broken the whole process down into 15 easy-to-follow chapters.

Take your time, don't rush through the book. Keep pen and paper handy.

This book is perfect if you want to start a non-fiction self-publishing business but are not a seasoned writer. You might be looking to create a second income or even want to focus on publishing full-time. I'm going to take you through all the stages involved, from having that initial idea to seeing your non-fiction book up there on the Amazon bookshelves.

You don't need to be a writer or a digital geek and you won't find any fancy jargon here to put you off. I'm going to give you the low-down in simple layman's terms so that you can begin your self-publishing adventure with a clear idea of what's involved.

Nowadays, anyone can publish a book and there's no reason why you can't.

Once you learn about the tools you need and you understand each step, it will be possible to earn a good income. In fact, in a fairly short period of time, you could turn it into a full-time enterprise.

Several of my colleagues are doing just that. Some of them have never made a penny online before in any online business and they were complete novices to begin with. It just goes to show you the power that self-publishing has.

After all, who doesn't like books?

I'll be showing you how to create a complete publishing business from scratch, not just how to write a one-off book. Think of it as an insider's guide on how to build a publishing empire that you can eventually sell for multiple six-figures if you wish.

How does that sound?

There is lot to cover, but I've got your back. As you go through this book, i've laid out everything you need to know about getting into the business, starting with ways of finding things to write about. It's not always easy to come up with a subject, so I'll be helping you learn how to narrow it down.

I'll also be talking about what keywords are and why they are so important when thinking of your book title, as well as how to find the best ones.

You'll learn how to write a manuscript, or get someone else to do it for you. Not everyone is good at writing, but you can still get a book written and I'll be telling you how.

When it comes to publishing on Amazon, you'll have to consider things such as formatting and getting a book cover designed first. We'll go through all of that in easy speak and you'll find it a lot less complicated than you initially thought.

I'll explain ways for you to get 5-star reviews so that your books do well in the Amazon ranking system and I'll also be sharing industry tips with you on the art of successful marketing. You can even learn about converting your paperback or hardback into an audiobook so that you have a foot in that market too.

You might have been dreaming of getting into publishing but were worried about the steep learning curve needed. It can seem overwhelming at first and there's always the fear of failure, right? Now, you don't have to worry because I'm here to show you how to do it. Think of this book as a course on self-publishing cheekily disguised as a book.

You don't need a massive amount of money to get started, but you can make a whole lot of it once you take off. You will need plenty of patience and be prepared to work hard at it, the rewards can be amazing.

Right. Are you ready?, let's get to work then!

P.S I have a great free gift waiting for you over at https://keith.subscribemenow.com/

1

SCRATCH THAT NICHE

When writing your non-fiction book, you are going to need to decide on a few things first before you write the actual manuscript. You may not have the title in mind at this point and that's OK, but you do need to know the subject you are going to write about.

I don't know about you but I love things to be simple. I can't stand anything that is overcomplicated. You will find everything in this book explained in a simple manner. I've tried to lay it all out in a logical sequence, with easy-to-follow steps.

Maybe on the first reading of this book, you might think "Stuff this, this self-publishing malarkey is Super Hard." I promise you it will get easier. If you are attempting self-publishing for the very first time, it might look a little difficult at first. I didn't say it was going to be easy, just simple.

I dare you, in fact, I double dare you to finish the entire book. And if you don't get it the first time around, read it again. BUT, promise me you'll take action.

Ok, let's get into it.

You need to write books about subjects that people care enough about, that they will actually go out and spend money to buy the book. This might sound obvious, but it's not.

Get to know who your audience is:

This book was written for people who want to learn how to create a self-publishing business. The buyer could be a male or a female from 16-95. The self publishing book audience is extremely large and diverse.

Many people just decide to write a book anyway, regardless of what competition there is for the subject, or indeed whether there is any demand for the book at all.

Once you have read this book, you will be in no doubt as to what the best topics to write about are.

You've picked up this book because you want to make money. I started this self-publishing business because I wanted to make money, NOT because I wanted to be a famous author and do book signings.

I would much rather be lying on a desert island watching my sales increase on Amazon than having to sit in local bookstores waiting for someone to ask me to sign their book. I built this business for the purpose of one thing only—freedom. And you can too.

Look at every book release as another stepping-stone toward your end goal, financial freedom. Each book is another piece of real estate, to get to your ultimate goal, it might take you 100 books, it might take 50, 25 or even just 1; no one knows.

That is the beauty of this business - it is full of surprises.

Whatever subject you decide to choose, there will always be some competition out there. That's OK. You want to avoid picking a subject that hardly anyone has ever heard of, especially if this is your first book. The goal at the end of the day is to create books that sell; books that people want. Then, you just keep repeating the process over and over again.

This is how you eventually build an Empire.

Right, let's go diving.

First of all, we are going to take a look at the top four broad non-fiction niches.

Once we have picked a broad niche to enter, we can then niche down even further to create a sub-niche. By niching down further and really specializing, we are then starting to focus on finding less competitive niches. In the self-publishing business, it's better to be a big fish in a small pond, than it is to be a small fish in a big pond.

Niching down simply means finding a niche within a niche (a sub-niche).

Before we start: You don't have to write about a subject that you particularly like or know a lot about, although it would help to do so. Many of my writing colleagues are writing about subjects that they had never thought about until they started writing books.

I know this goes against all conventional advice. However, I've found that if you limit yourself to just writing about subjects you know about, you are indeed limiting yourself.

Of course, if you are an SEO expert or a caterer, or someone passionate about blogging, niche down and find some cool subjects within those niches to write about.

I'm just saying that you don't have to.

You can do all the research you need online for any subject you care to write about, and write about anything you like. You don't have to be an expert, you just need to know more than most people. People buy non-fiction books to get answers to their problems. They often don't have the time themselves to spend hours and hours scouring the Internet.

This is where you come in.

You give them all the answers they need in your book.

Although I am talking about the four main niches here, plenty of people are making money from books that don't fall within these top four, which is fine as long as there is a market for the subject.

More on that, later.

The Top Four Broad Niches (in no particular order) are:

1. Money

2. Health & Wellness

3. Relationships

4. Hobbies

Our aim is to find a topic that we can write about within one of the above broad niches. Let's say for example you choose Health & Wellness.

There are multiple topics we can write about within the Health & Wellness niche. It is hugely popular.

In 2021 GLOBE NEWSWIRE reported: The global health and wellness market size was estimated at **USD 4,436.1 billion in 2020**. The huge rise of chronic diseases among the world population is the key driver of the global health and wellness market.

Choose a niche where there is plenty of money floating around.

Let's look at Dieting & Losing Weight. We know that people buy plenty of books on this subject. You just have to go to Amazon.com and look at their book categories for Health, Fitness & Dieting. If you type the word "Dieting" into the search box, this alone will bring up around 50,000 results.

If we niche down even further, we could write about Dieting >Keto Diet. Or we could dive even further into this niche and look at Dieting>Keto Diet>For Women Over 50.

We are looking for potential topics that can be profitable for us without huge competition. I am assuming you want to write more than one book, so look for topics that have multiple sub-topics within that niche. You can then write many different books.

For example,

Book 1. Keto Diet for Women over 50

Book 2. Keto Diet for men

Book 3. Keto Diet Recipes for Teens on The Go

Book 4. Keto Diet For Animals (Just Kidding)

Now, I'm not suggesting doing books on the Keto diet. I'm just showing you how to deep dive into a subject to pick some possible winning topics.

Let's go fishing.

To get some idea on which book topics are popular, we first need to go to Amazon.com. I've chosen Amazon.com as it is the largest of all the Amazon sites and serves the most people.

Go to books/best sellers

https://www.Amazon.com/gp/bestsellers/books

You will see a menu on the left-hand side of all the main categories. For instance, if you click on business and money, you will see the current best sellers on the topic of business and money. Keep scrolling down. Can you see any topics that you could write a book on?. We know the subject is popular or it wouldn't be on the best-sellers list.

Let's say that you see several books on "habits". We don't have to just copy everyone else and write a book on habits. Look at the competition. Let's be different; we know that "habits' sells well but what problems do people have within the "habit" niche?

Maybe their habits are:

1. They are terrible with money

2. They can't seem to get motivated

3. They procrastinate a lot

4. They have low self-esteem

5. They start things, but never finish them

6. They are habitual nail-biters

7. They avoid people, they have no or very low social skills

I think you get the point. You don't have to just create a book about "habits", you can create several books on "specific habits".

Ideas are everywhere and there is a huge thirst for information. People have problems, lots of them, and it's our job to write books on solving those problems. We don't have to limit our research to Amazon only - there are plenty of other places on the Internet that you can find good book topics.

Where do people go to talk about their problems?

1. Forums

2. Quora

3. Social Media.

Forums

People often think that forums are so "last decade", but if you are looking for book ideas, these dinosaurs are very useful. You simply type into Google your broad category followed by the word "forum"

For instance, to find forums catering for people interested in Health & Wellness, simply type in Health & Wellness forums..

Google will then magically come up with a ton of forums in your broad niche. Join one or two for free and listen. You will soon see the same problems coming up again and again.

These problems may be ones that you can write a book about.

Back in 2011, I used to write a blog called "Keith's Money Making Tips". I know, cheesy, eh? I would create a new tip every day and link the blog post to an affiliate product. I would get most of my ideas from a forum called the Warrior Forum.

What has this got to do with books?

Think of a forum as mental stimuli. If you spend enough time listening, you'll never run out of book ideas. This is the beauty of creating non-fiction. Just one problem can be enough to write an entire book about. And as we know, people never have just one problem.

BTW, Keith's Money Making Tips is now long gone, but it got me started writing. Blogging is good practice for writing books as it gets you into writing mode and it doesn't need to be something long or complicated.

Quora

This is a crazy website. Quora.com is a website where people go just to get their questions answered. Someone asks a question and people dive in with their answers. You would be surprised at how many people are more than willing to give their opinion and use their expertise to answer weird questions. Think of the response you could get if you are thinking of writing a book on "habits".

Imagine asking questions like:

What is your most annoying habit?

What habits annoy you the most in people?

You would probably be overwhelmed by the response and also learn a lot you probably didn't know about the subject.

The potential of Quora for getting ideas is unlimited. It's one of my favourite places to get ideas for books.

Social Media

We all know people like a good old moan, but Social Media can be also be very useful for research. Remember, we are selling books to humans, not monkeys. Therefore, we need to go where humans hang out. And there are lots of them (and monkeys) on Social Media.

Facebook

I know there are a lot of people who just don't like Facebook.

A very large part of the world hangs out on Facebook. Whether you are PRO or ANTI Facebook, my recommendation to you is to start getting friendly with Facebook once more, as you can leverage the good people of Facebook to do useful research and also to help you out in the future when you publish your books.

Facebook friends can become real friends. I've teamed up with some wonderful people on Facebook.

A good place to start is a Facebook group. Let's say you have an inkling to write a book about Habits, yes, habits AGAIN!!. If you type in the word 'habits' into the Facebook search bar, you can see groups on "Habits of Health", Habits of Hope, Habits for Success".

You simply join the group and listen in to the questions, and the answers. This (over time) will give you the material you need to base your book on. Also, you now have access to a lot of group members who are interested in this particular subject.

It is possible to leverage those members at a later date to be either reviewers or maybe even buyers of your book. Think outside the box. More on this in a later chapter.

Key Points

• Keep things simple. Self-Publishing may not seem easy at first, but after you've written your first book, it will get a lot easier. Be prepared for some hard work and frustration initially.

• Select a broad niche, one of the top 4, to start off with.

• Do extensive research to find out what people's problems actually are within those top 4 broad niches.

• Get friendly with Facebook. I know a lot of people either don't like Facebook or think that it's a total waste of time, but you really can use Facebook to your advantage, both for research and for getting reviews on your books in the future.

- Start getting social media-friendly. You will need as many channels as possible to market your book. There are many other social channels out there besides Facebook. - Twitter, LinkedIn, Pinterest, YouTube, TikTok and Instagram are also very popular.

SIDE-NOTE: I recently had a business customer purchase 175 copies of one of my books. She found me on Instagram.

2
THE MAGIC OF KEYWORDS

Can you sell books without putting keywords in the title? You can, but I wouldn't advise it. Not having keywords in your title or book description is a bit like flying a plane by the seat of your pants. You might make it, you might not.

Keywords are very important if you want people to find your books. Buyers go on to Amazon and they search for specific things. We need to get our book titles in with a winning chance of being found. We do this by adding keywords to the title, the subtitle, and the book description on Amazon.

Many authors skip over this point entirely and just go ahead and publish their book without any thought to optimizing it for the Amazon search engine. This is a serious mistake. If you do this, people will probably only find your book by chance and with so many books on the Amazon website, you really are making it a lottery.

Of course, some people already have a massive following. They could be influencers with large email lists or people who have a huge presence on Instagram, In that case, they may only need to mention to their following that they've published a new book on Amazon and the masses will buy it. But for most people, this really isn't the case and we need to work on getting our books seen.

You are are about to become a self-publisher now, this involves wearing a few different hats. You are not just the author, you are also the creator, the manager and the marketer too. We need our title to at least contain the main keyword, and also, where possible in our subtitle. (The subtitle tends to be a short description of our book).

A keyword is the same as our chosen topic. "Self publishing for beginners" is a topic and a long-tail keyword. A long-tail keyword tends to be a phrase of four words or more, whereas a short-tail keyword contains three words or less. The shorter the keyword, the more competitive it tends to be.

For example, when I wrote a book on how to write a book, I simply titled it **"How To Write A Book".** This keyword gets straight to the point and was a popular long-tail keyword that people were typing into Amazon at the time.

My subtitle was **" The Beginner's Guide To Writing A Non-Fiction Book For Fun And Profit"**. This was not the best subtitle in the world, it does have one decent keyword (non-fiction book) although that is a bit broad, but it does get straight to the point and describes what the book is about.

Keep it simple. Don't make the potential buyer work too hard to buy your book. We want to create a simple pathway from the buyer to your buy button.

Also, don't cram your titles with keywords. This is called keyword stuffing. Not only does it look terrible, but it may also be flagged up by Amazon if you do that. The title, subtitle and description should all make sense

Step 1.

AMZ Suggestion Expander

Below, I am using a free tool called AMZ suggestion expander. It's a free chrome extension that expands and shows you many other suggestions for the keyword you type in.

Look what happens when I type the word Habits into the Amazon search bar.

It doesn't give the volume of searches on Amazon, but it is a great start. There are paid tools out there to find the search volume of a keyword. However some of these tools, like "Publisher Rocket", are quite pricey and cost around $100.

I tend to use the free version of "Semrush", which gives you 10 free searches a day. This gives you an idea of how popular the keyword is on the Internet (not Amazon). You can find out more about Semrush from the link below.

https://www.semrush.com/analytics/keywordmagic/start

Knowing how popular this keyword is universally is valuable information, as people could potentially find your book through Google. Having a book on a high-traffic site like Amazon with good search engine optimization could potentially attract many more sales from people who were just searching for that specific keyword on the internet.

You now have an idea of what people are looking for when searching "habits". This keyword in itself is very broad, so niche down within the habit niche and keep going until you come up with an array of potential topics.

Step 2.

KDSPY

When I first started publishing books, I was determined not to spend a lot of money on software. However, I did buy KDSPY. You don't have to have this, but it will save you a lot of work.

What is KDSPY?

KDSPY is **a time-saving research companion** that allows authors to find profitable book ideas, and Amazon categories & keywords. You can research your competition, your potential niche markets, categories, keywords, and title ideas.

Check out KDSPY here.

https://keitheverett.co.uk/kdspy

Once you have added the KDSPY chrome extension to your Google browser, you will want to view potentially profitable searches in "incognito mode". This is because your Amazon account is personal to you, it cookies you into your searches and we don't want Amazon influencing our searches.

This is quite simple to do. In the top right-hand side of your chrome browser you have three dots (update), click that and select "new incognito window". You will also need to select the extension itself under "extensions" and select "allow in incognito".

This is what incognito mode looks like:

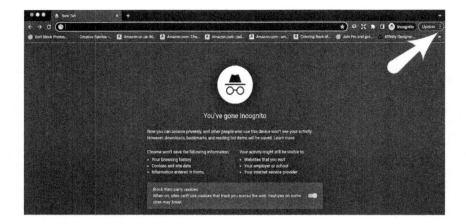

KDSPY will give you the following information for the keywords you type into it. It will list 20 books that currently rank for that keyword.

1. It will give you each book's seller rank. **The lower this is, the better** (I'll explain this shortly).

2. It will tell you how many pages your competitor's books have.

3. It will tell you the price, the estimated amount of monthly sales, the estimated monthly revenue, and the number of reviews each book has.

Once you are in incognito mode, type in Amazon.com (always use this for this process). Click on the dropdown list on the search bar and select "books". Then type in your keyword. In this case, we are using the keyword "Habits For Teens"

NEXT: click on the little KDSPY icon at the top right of your browser.

You now have a list of the top 20 books competing for that keyword.

If you are listening to this book on Audible, all images are included in the accompanying free pdf.

The image above shows the average sales rank, the average monthly revenue, the average price, and the average number of reviews.

When I choose a keyword to base my book's content and title on I like to see the average sales rank below 300,000. I like to see the average monthly revenue above $1000, and I like to see at least 4 or 5 books with a sales rank (far right column) below 30,000.

This is just a guide.

The above example is a little bit high on the average sales rank. It's perfect for the average monthly revenue. The 20 books listed are averaging $2260 (gross) per month. There are 4 books below 30,000 sales rank in the right-hand column. So that is fine, (don't count the books showing Zero).

Also, when you do this, you may pick up an outlier. This is a book showing an exceptionally high sales rank compared to all the others. If this is so, just "untick" it in the right-hand column to reset the overall figures.

This might sound terribly complicated, but think how complicated it would be if you had to figure all this out in your head. This tool saves you hours of research and it's worth every penny, in my view.

Sales Rank V BSR (Best Sellers Rank)

One big thing that a lot of new sellers confuse when they first start selling on Amazon is the difference between Amazon Best Sellers Rank and organic ranking. Your **BSR is how well the product ranks based on sales** while the organic ranking (**sales rank**) is how well the product ranks in search for a given keyword.

I hope this chapter has clarified the need to apply keywords into your calculations when deciding on a topic and title. It is a little complicated at first but as you progress through your self-publishing journey, it does get much easier.

Key Points

• Keywords are very important in deciding both the viability of your topic and how you portray your title and subtitle.

• If you only ever purchase one piece of keyword software, make it KDSPY. This has saved me literally hundreds of hours of work in the past.

• Don't get confused over sales rank and best sellers rank. The sales rank is a number that determines how well a product is ranking for a specific keyword. The Bestsellers rank (#BSR) is seen on every product listing on Amazon. It shows you how well or how badly a product is selling at that moment. The lower the number, the better.

❊ 3 ❊
CREATING THAT AMAZING MANUSCRIPT

Once you've decided on the topic you want to write about and done your keyword research search for the title and subtitle, it's time to crack on with the actual manuscript.

If you feel that you are a reasonably good writer, that's great. If this part of the process is putting you off because you feel you don't have the time, or inclination to do it, I'll be talking later on about how to get someone to write your book for you.

But, this is your first book, so have a go at writing it yourself.

Choosing your weapons

Let's say that you use a laptop or PC and want to begin writing. Whatever device you have, you will find inbuilt software programs for creating documents. The two most common ones are Microsoft Word and Google Docs. Both enable you to create, edit, and save what you write onto your laptop/PC, as well as on the virtual cloud.

You can also share these documents as attachments (if you wish) via email or any online messaging app.

Whether you use Google Docs or Microsoft Word, it's entirely up to you. Think of them both as blank pages you fill with text that also let you choose from a range of writing tools as you do so. Some writers swear by Word but I've used Google Docs too and there isn't that much difference between them for the purpose of writing our book.

When you start creating your document, you can select the style and size of the font you are going to use, set the page layout and add margins, headers, images, graphs... whatever you want. A basic manuscript is usually mostly text, so that's what I'll be focusing on here. You can also check out some online editing software that has been designed specifically for writers such as Scrivener, or Ulysses for Macs.

The good ones don't come free, so you will need to decide if you really need them or not. You are talking anything from $20 a month to $150, which can take up a large part of your budget. There are some good free software options like FastPencil and FocusWriter, although they work better if you are more into fiction writing. Like everything in life, more advanced features come as paid upgrades and it's useful to bear that in mind.

If you aren't sure what software you want to use to create your document, here are some things to look out for:

• Does it have a steep learning curve or can you get the hang of it easily?

• Is it distraction-free or is the template too busy and cluttered?

• Does it come with auto-save so you never run the risk of losing your hard work in the event of a PC crash or power outage?

• Does it offer free cloud storage?

• Does it include built-in sharing tools for when you want to share the file with someone else?

• Does it give you too many confusing options?

• Is it too complicated to understand?

• Does it come with useless extras that you'll never use like advanced HTML and character tracking?

You don't want to shoot yourself in the foot at the first hurdle by trying to work with something too complex, so stick to what you feel most comfortable with. All you basically need is a blank screen page to write on with your keyboard. Any formatting issues can be dealt with later.

Working online

It's a good idea to work online so that anything you write is continuously being backed up and saved to the cloud, which is a virtual storage space offered by the server. Both Google Drive and OneDrive offer the same basic features for storing your online work. If you have a Google account, for example, you can go to Google Drive and once there, select the **New** feature on the top left-hand side of the screen.

After you have selected it, a drop-down menu gives you several options. Choose **Google Docs** and a brand new document will open for you in another window. Add a title straight away and this file will automatically be saved online in your Google Drive. You can also download it to your PC or laptop by moving your mouse to the top left-hand side of the toolbar and selecting **File>Download**. It will ask you where you want it to be saved and that's it.

You can continue to work online and there is also an option to work offline if you don't have an internet connection. Everything you write down can be saved on the Drive later when you are re-connected.

Spend some time familiarizing yourself with the top toolbar of the document you are working on in Google Docs or Microsoft Word until you have found your bearings. If you get stuck or aren't sure how to use something, you can always go to the help section you will find by selecting the question mark icon (?) in the top left-hand corner.

Keep your work organized by creating folders for each project. For example, on Google Drive, select New from the top left-hand corner again and then click on Folder in the drop-down menu. You'll be asked to name your folder and once you've done that, you can add files to it as you go along.

Get your thoughts in order

Once you have created a new file, it's time to type. You will have decided on your book title by now and the next step is to create an outline of what your book is going to include. You'll need to spend some time thinking about this beforehand.

Ask yourself things like:

→ What topic you will cover, in one sentence

→ Why readers will find it useful/interesting

→ Who the book is for (age/occupation/interest group, etc.)

→ What the reader wants to know

→ How you can help them or provide useful information

→ How you are going to divide the chapters

→ How many words it will be

Don't forget that a non-fiction book is supposed to inform the reader so you need a clear outline of how you are going to do that before you start adding flesh to the bones. Your outline should look something like this:

• The main topic

• The purpose of the book (see above)

• The structure - is it a problem/answer, compare/contrast, step-by-step guide?

• Divide your main points into different chapters

• Add a summary of what will be included in each one

Once you've finished your outline, use it as the framework for your writing. You can always tweak it further down the road if you want to. The more often you go through this process, the better you will become at getting it right and it's a very useful habit to adopt from day one.

Make a table of contents

Every non-fiction book has a table of contents, which tells the reader what to expect in each chapter. As for the number of chapters you should include, anything from 5 to 15 is OK. I usually aim for ten, but this will vary from book to book. I also include an introduction and conclusion, just like in this book.

Let's say you have decided to write a book about how to find a job online. I'm sure you already have a great idea of what you want to say after doing the outline. Now, you need to break things up into distinct chapters that focus on different aspects of searching for a job online. Your table of contents (TOC) might look something like this:

Book title

How To Find A Job Online

Introduction

Introduce the topic, say why you are qualified to talk about it, and explain what the readers can expect to learn from your book.

Chapter 1

Today's trends. Talk about what skills are in high demand and how to get yourself noticed.

Chapter 2

Jobs on the internet. Inform your reader about the choice of online jobs and where to find them.

Chapter 3

Time for your C.V. Explain the importance of an updated resume and how to make one from scratch.

Chapter 4

Get that job. Give the reader tips on how to apply for a job and what to watch out for when making the application.

Chapter 5

Digital job brokers. Tell the reader about different job platforms, such as Fiverr, and lay out the pros and cons.

Chapter 6

Upskilling online. Talk about the availability of online courses, seminars, and long-distance learning.

Chapter 7

Startups from scratch. Talk about the benefits of forming a startup and what kind of help and investment is available.

Chapter 8

Remote/Hybrid working. Go through ways to establish new working patterns for better work/life balance.

Chapter 9

An action plan. How to make a plan for the next 6 or 12 months to secure the job you want.

Chapter 10

The perfect portfolio. How to create an impressive portfolio if your industry sector requires it.

Conclusion

A brief recap of the information in the above chapters.

Once you have your "table of contents" in place, it's a lot easier to start writing. You know exactly what will go into each chapter so there's much less danger of repeating yourself or missing out on anything important. If you don't do a table of contents, the likelihood is that you'll just start writing down whatever pops into your head and you'll soon find that you will run out of steam or get lost along the way.

Hot tip: *Whenever a book is displayed on the Amazon page, the 'Look inside' feature allows buyers to check out the first few pages, including the Table of Contents. Make sure it has catchy chapter titles to grab the reader's attention and make them want to buy!*

Worrying about word count

Although there's no limitation on how long your non-fiction book should be for Amazon, I recommend that you start at a minimum of 30,000 words. That's about 3,000 words for each chapter, give or take. If you want to convert your manuscript to an Audiobook later on, you should definitely make sure it is at least 32,000 words. This will give you over 3hrs of Audio.

But, I digress.

If you have written 30,000 words, your book will have around 130 pages when it's printed, which is a reasonable size. If you also offer it as an ebook (more about that later), then the number of pages isn't that clear-cut because it depends on how the reader uses Kindle. They might enlarge the fonts, for example, for an easier reading experience.

Doing your homework

It's a good idea to do your research before you start to work through each chapter. You might be highly qualified in a particular subject but should still back up what you know, you don't want to write something that isn't true or correct.

Read up on your subject, get your facts right, and be spot on with the details. Your book will flop big time if it includes incorrect information and you've done sloppy research.

I want to stress something here: You don't need to be an expert in a particular field to write about it. If, for example, your keyword search has led you to want to write about herbal remedies, you **DON'T** need to be a botanist! What you **DO NEED** is to research the topic as much as you can and use reliable sources.

And remember don't copy anything word for word. Use information to give you your own ideas.

There's limitless information on the internet about every subject under the sun, and plenty of experts talking about them. To find reliable sources where you can discover useful information for your book, go to Google search, or any other browser and type in a few keywords.

For example, sticking with the herbal remedies theme, type in the words 'herbal remedies'. You'll immediately see blogs, books, videos, and images on the subject. Scroll down to check out any interesting articles and also look at the list of commonly asked questions that will appear further down the screen. These will each take you to a new browser window, with more details on every aspect of herbal remedies.

You can spend hours and hours reading through online sources about the topic and you should make notes as you do so. Using what you've learned, you can slowly start to create content for each chapter. A **BIG** word of warning here though - copying someone else's work (plagiarism) is illegal and could get you into serious trouble. Make sure that everything you write is unique and in your own words. If you do want to quote somebody, you need to mention the source either in brackets or as a footnote. A lot of books also include a 'Sources' section at the end, which gives details about who said what.

Hot tip: *If you want to make sure your book is 100% plagiarism-free, use software like Copyscape or Grammarly, which will scan the text and give you a report of what might be a direct copy-paste from another source.*

Creating your manuscript

Start each chapter by presenting the theme of what you will be talking about, adding useful information as you proceed. When you have written a few paragraphs, go back to the beginning and read them over. Are they easy to understand? Do they make sense? Are they interesting?

This is probably the most difficult part of the whole book-writing process and it can take some time to get the hang of. Imagine that you are the reader who expects to learn something specific - are you giving them what they want to know? You can continue writing the rest of the chapter until you reach the end, re-reading every couple of paragraphs as you go. This also helps you to keep on track and not wander off the subject.

Once you are happy with your writing, you will need to check for spelling, typos, and grammatical errors. If you want, you can leave this until the whole book is complete, but I prefer to do it as I go.

Checking for errors

Not everyone is good at writing and even seasoned authors have editors and proofreaders who check their work for them. You might be unsure about spelling, punctuation, grammar, or anything else, and need help with that. Luckily, there are a lot of great free tools you can use. The most obvious one is the spell checker on your Google Docs or Microsoft Word toolbar.

On Docs:

- Select the **Tools** tab at the top of your screen.

- You'll see the option for spelling and grammar.

- Click on that and make sure the 3 options for **spelling and grammar check**, **spelling suggestions**, and **grammar suggestions** are activated.

- Choose **spelling and grammar check.**

- You will automatically see a pop-up box that gives you a wrongly-spelled word and a suggestion, which you can either accept or ignore.

On Word:

- Press the **F7** key on your keyboard or follow these steps:

- Click on the **Review** tab.

- Select **Spelling** or **Spelling & Grammar**.

- A dialogue box will pop up with any misspelled words which you can ignore or change.

Both of the above are handy tools for catching typos but nothing beats reading your writing carefully. The spell checks don't always catch words that might be easily confused, such as *there* and *their*. You might see words being highlighted or underlined in red if you have enabled the spelling suggestions. You can change them if you like and also see suggestions when you hover over the word with your mouse.

As well as that, you need to make sure you have selected the right language settings. There is a difference between American English and

UK English, (such as the use of the word color and colour). Depending on what language you want to use, go to settings on this particular document and select the right language preference for your book.

Editing software

When you want to do a check on your grammar, you can use one of the free software tools on the market. Grammarly is the most well-known, although there are a lot of others you can use such as Ginger, Scribens, Hemingway, ProWritingAid, and more. Some of them are free to use online and most offer premium benefits for monthly subscriptions.

These AI editing tools are a godsend for those of us who are useless at grammar and they can pick up on tiny typos too, such as extra spaces or the incorrect use of a comma. All you need to do is copy your text and drop it in the allocated box of your chosen software and it will scan it for possible mistakes. Don't forget to correct your original Doc or Word file, because the software is only looking at the text you copied and not your original file.

I strongly suggest you exercise common sense when using these editing aids. They aren't always right and often make suggestions that we would never use in real life. Here again, a good old-fashioned pair of eyes are way better than any software, although they can be a useful addition to your toolbox.

Hot tip: *You can listen to what you have written to see how it sounds using a text-to-speech (TTS) tool. On Microsoft Word, you can add this speak command to your Quick Access Toolbar by clicking on Customize Quick Access Toolbar>More Commands>All Commands>Speak>Add>OK. For Google Docs, go to Add-Ons>Read Aloud>Open Sidebar. If you don't see the option for Read Aloud, you can search for the extension and download it by selecting Get More Add-Ons.*

A second pair of eyes

When I wrote my first book, "Money Mind Crush", the only tool I used was Google Docs. I wasn't aware of the alternatives and it took me forever to get it right. Ever since then, I've made sure I use all the help out there I can to catch any errors or typos and to save time.

You do have the option of paying for a **developmental editor** to go through the text and make sure its structure is sound and that it all flows seamlessly. They might also do the **line editing** for you, which is basically checking that each sentence is grammatically correct in terms of syntax, word order, etc.

It's also a very good idea to hire a **proofreader,** who will go through it with a fine-tooth comb, spotting all the tiny errors you've overlooked such as extra spacing, and so on. These are people with expertise and will have much more experience than you at checking manuscripts before publishing so they are definitely worth the investment.

Hire a freelancer

If you want to build a successful publishing business but don't want to get bogged down with the nitty-gritty of writing, you can hire a ghostwriter. This is someone who writes on a work-to-hire basis and will write your book for you when you tell them what you want. There are plenty of good writers out there on freelancer websites such as Fiverr and Upwork.

The beauty of this is that you can agree on a fixed price, set a deadline for when the work should be ready, and you only need to pay them when it has been submitted. You can even ask them to sign a **Non Disclosure Agreement to protect your intellectual property.** This means that they can't run off with your book and publish it themselves so remember to put that in the contract.

Formatting for publication

When you are happy with your manuscript and ready to publish it, you need to go through one more stage. This is the formatting process, which turns your work from a text document into a book format. There are people out there who can do it for you for a price, but I've found some great software that makes it super easy to do myself.

Vellum is one of those, and all you need to do is download the program. Then, drop your manuscript into the application and it will magically transform it into a proper book layout. You can tweak it to your liking, changing the style of the font, headers, etc. It can seem expensive to buy, at around $250, but it's a one-off payment that can save you a lot of headaches.

At the time of my writing this book, Vellum is only available for Mac users so if you are using something else, I would recommend that you go to Kindle Direct Publishing and download Kindle Create. This is a free software app and, just like Vellum, allows you to change your document into a book layout. When you've tinkered around with it until you are happy, you can then save it and export the whole file straight to the KDP website and upload it onto their Amazon bookshelf.

Don't forget your book cover

On Amazon, customers judge a book by its cover, so it needs to grab their attention. It doesn't matter how great your book is: if the cover is naff, no one is likely to buy it. I strongly recommend that you hire a professional book cover creator to do the work for you and, here again, you'll find plenty of talent on platforms like Fiverr and Upwork. Check out their portfolios and compare pricing until you find someone that you think is suitable for your book and budget.

You will need to have what's called the **book blurb** ready to send to the designer. This is a short text that goes on the back cover of the book and is like a teaser of what's inside.

For your Amazon page

You should also write an attractive description of your book that will persuade readers to buy it. You can create some kind of author profile if you like as well, whether you are using a real name or a pen name. The aim is to get customers to spend money on YOUR book. Make it as appealing as possible so that it stands out from the crowd.

Write a book in less than six weeks

To get your business up and running, you need to be productive. That means getting as many books out there as you can, in the fastest time possible. Your book is a product and the sooner it's on the shelves, the better. It is doable if you are prepared to put in the time and energy.

It only takes two hours of writing a day to complete a 30,000-word book in six weeks or under. That's only around 700 words a day for 42 days. Allocate that time to doing nothing but writing each day. Get rid of any distractions while you do so like phone notifications and always set a timer. Don't get up until you've worked for two hours, unless nature calls, of course ! Once you get into the habit of writing like this, you'll soon pick up speed and be even more productive.

Key Points

• Choose your weapons - Google Docs or Microsoft Word.

• Do your research before you begin writing.

• Get your thoughts in order, create the structure of your book, let your outline deliver the book in a logical order.

• Don't forget to get your work edited before publishing. Preferably by a professional editor.

• Make sure your cover stands out. People DO judge a book by its cover.

4
HIRE A GHOSTWRITER OR DO IT YOURSELF?

You may think that hiring a Ghostwriter to write your books is a CRAZY expense. After all, why pay for a Ghostwriter when you can do the work yourself and save a packet, right?

Wrong.

Think of why you are going into the self-publishing business in the first place. Is it because you want to be an Author, or is it because you want to make money and maybe build an empire? Of course, the answer could be **BOTH**.

Here is my take on this:

To get a half-decent Ghostwriter on Upwork, you would probably need to pay around $1000 to get a 30,000-word book written. You can get it done cheaper but I suggest going for quality over price. Start as you mean to go on and always deliver a quality book.

You might think that $1000 is a huge expense for your digital real estate but look at the possible earning potential from that one book.

A $1000 Ghostwritten book could end up making you $1000 a month (or more), in the future. I'm not saying it will, I'm just saying it could. How a book performs on Amazon greatly depends on the work YOU put into it with the outline, the quality of the writer, plus the work that you do after publishing to promote it.

The Ghostwriter can only produce a book as good as the outline you give them. If you give them a poor outline with very little information in it, you can't expect your Ghostwriter to perform miracles and write you a best-selling book.

This is what I do.

I have a Ghostwriter who writes several of my books. I also write books myself. This usually means that I tend to have a new book out each month. The more books you add to the mix, the more potential profits you will have, and therefore the more books you can afford to give your Ghostwriter to write.

In the first year of being in the self-publishing business, I didn't take one cent in profit for myself. I simply put the earnings back into the business to be able to afford to have a new book written each month.

I also make sure that I have the best cover I can afford ($200) and when the book is complete, I send it off to a narrator to have it appear as an audiobook on Audible. My narrator charges me $100 per finished hour, this equates to around $300 for a 30,000 word book.

So, my total cost for a book that I don't write myself is around $1500. If I write it myself I pay $500 approximately for the cover and the narration and around $100 for editing making it a total of $650.

Here's where it gets interesting

At first, it's all pay out. This is a typical situation whenever you start any new business. I have been creating businesses for over 40 years now. Most businesses don't make much in the first year, some lose money or may break even. It does take patience. With the self-publishing business, it's pretty much the same. Even if you are making money, put it back into the business. You want to have as many top-notch books out there on Amazon as possible.

Notice I say "top-notch" books. Books that have longevity tend to be books that are well written and solve a person's problem. People don't want to spend their hard-earned cash on fluff. If you give people a good book, many will give you a good review.

There is always the exception though, you can produce a brilliant book and some idiot will come along and give you a 1 star review.

When you have plenty of good reviews, this will drive sales to your book. Make no mistake: if you write a low-quality book, the readers will let you know about it in no uncertain terms with bad reviews.

You want to still be making sales this year, next year, and for as long as possible. Start off by dripping any profit back into production and advertising costs. I haven't mentioned Amazon ads yet, we'll talk about that a little later on.

So, is it worth getting a Ghostwriter?. A definite YES from me. I like being an author, I love writing books but BOY, a good Ghostwriter can make all the difference to your self-publishing business. Invest in a good writer, but I also recommend that you also write some of your books.

Don't worry if money is a bit tight at the moment and you can't afford a Ghostwriter. This book is all about learning to do it yourself. So far, I have explained how to find the ideas for your book, and how to find those KILLER keywords. I've also explained how to create your own manuscript.

Even if you decide to use a Ghostwriter in the future, I would always recommend that you create your very first book yourself. It's important that you know and understand the process.

There are quite a few pieces to the self-publishing puzzle but don't worry, this book is about creating a self-publishing business, not just a one-off book.

Once you become proficient at this you will find it one of the most enjoyable, and potentially profitable businesses on the Internet. You can create real generational wealth in self-publishing and NO, that's not Internet blarney. It's a fact. Several of my colleagues have created five-figure MONTHLY incomes from self-publishing.

Not all books go on to make money. But if you are selecting the right topics, giving people the answers to their problems, creating nice book covers that really stand out, and using good keywords in your titles and descriptions, there is no reason at all why your books cannot go on to make a decent income month after month, year after year.

Facts:

Some books won't make much at all.

Some books will make a small amount each month.

Some books will make some fairly decent returns each month.

And some books will go like **gangbusters!**

Here's why.

The Pareto Principle

I talk about the Pareto principle a lot in previous books of mine and there is a reason for this. I think this principle, once understood, can make a huge difference to how we perceive things. Not just in book publishing, but in life itself.

Wilfredo Pareto was an Italian Economist and Sociologist born in 1848. He came up with the principle that back in his home country of Italy, approximately 80% of his country's wealth was owned by 20% of the population.

This principle seems to work well today, as 80% of your results will come from around 20% of your efforts. It's not an exact science, but once we know which 20% is getting the most results, it makes sense to concentrate on that section a lot more.

This applies very much to the books that you create. If you create 10 books, possibly 2 of those books will create 80% of your revenue.

This is a golden opportunity to create more books in a similar vein. Using the Pareto principle for creating books is something that more authors should look at as it's a good guide on how to steer your publishing company towards more profit in the future.

When you do decide to find a ghostwriter, there are several companies online advertising writing services. Personally, I went straight to Upwork.com.

You will find that there are many writers on Upwork to suit all budgets. However, like everything in life, you tend to get what you pay for. Don't be tempted by ghostwriters offering super-cheap prices. Look for a ghostwriter that you feel offers good work at a fair price. Ask your ghostwriter for samples of their work so that you can see if they have what you are looking for. You can also hop on a Zoom call and interview them if you wish.

Remember: you are building a possible long-term relationship here. Treat your ghostwriter with respect, pay them on time and be fair with them. In return, you will have a valuable ally for a long time to come.

Key Points

• A Ghostwriter can only produce a good book if your outline is good. The more information you provide, the better

• Always write the first book yourself. This gives you a good grounding in what is required to create a good book.

• To build an Empire, write books yourself whilst getting books created by a ghostwriter. This means that you can produce many more books per year than if you wrote them all yourself.

• Remember the Pareto principle. Don't just write one book and hope for the best. Create many books. Some will probably SUCK, but others will do you proud and make money.

5
SHOULD I USE A PEN NAME OR REAL NAME?

Remember earlier on when I said not to overcomplicate things? Believe it or not, a lot of people get stuck on the subject of pen names.

A pen name is just another name that you decide to use as the author of your books.

Why would anyone want to do this?

Many books, famous or not, have been written by authors using pen names. There are many reasons for this. Perhaps an author's name is extremely hard to spell, maybe their name is a tad embarrassing, or perhaps that author just wants more privacy.

Perhaps they don't want their family to know that they are writing books. Another reason could be that they are writing books in several different niches and want to avoid any crossover.

Maybe you want to be well known in a particular niche, such as "Wallpapering and Tiling", but you also want to write books on Cryptocurrency. This could confuse a lot of people.

One minute you are known as the "Wallpaper and Tiling" expert, then you are known as the "Cryptocurrency expert". You can see how your followers might get confused.

BTW. I really recommend that you get good in one particular niche first. Write several books within that niche before branching out to others.

Other reasons for and against pen names

When I started writing books, I used my own name. I'm very proud of my books and being an author is a very respectful profession. Obviously, it depends on the sort of books you want to write.

I tend to write "self-help" and "how-to" books. I connect very well with this type of book and its audience and feel comfortable putting my name on the cover.

After a short while, I wanted to write a book where the subject matter was very much female-orientated. I knew that to create this type of book, I really needed someone who understood the subject matter from a female perspective.

This is why I chose a female ghostwriter and a pen name for that particular book. The book was fairly successful, so I asked my ghostwriter to write other books in the same genre under that pen name. My advice here is: if you are a male and you want to write a book that would be read mainly by females, DON'T pretend you are a female. Your female readers will see straight through it.

And vice versa.

Don't overcomplicate this. Many people in the arts industry use pen names. Many actors choose to use more user-friendly names. There is nothing wrong with using a pen name, you're not deceiving anyone, you're just simply using a name more suitable for either privacy reasons or because it's a "better fit" for that niche. Some of the most well-known authors use at least one pen name, depending on what type of book they are putting out there.

Getting reviews using a pen name

This is something that is often viewed as a problem. You might be wondering how you can ask for reviews when you are using a pen name.

Here's what I do.

On Facebook, I simply tell people up-front that I'm using a ghost-writer. I tell them it's more appropriate for the subject matter that I engage a writer for this purpose. You just have to be transparent about what you are doing.

There is a whole chapter on marketing and getting reviews later in this book so I won't go too much into it here. I do want to stress, though, that getting reviews is no harder if you are using a pen name than it is if you're using your own name.

With a pen name, you are creating a completely different persona. Because of that, you do need to use a little bit of poetic license here and there. You don't need to lie and invent qualifications for your pen name (please don't do that) it may feel a bit awkward to some people at first to take on this new persona. Here's how to deal with that:

The awkward bits

You are given an author profile when you publish a book on Amazon. This usually contains space for an author bio and a picture. So, if you are using a pen name, how do you do this?

Amazon has set up your author profile so that you can have several pen names. That's because Amazon realizes the importance of pen names and therefore helps you to achieve this.

Once you have published your first book on Amazon (I will show you how to do this later), you can set up your author profile here:

https://author.Amazon.com/home

Let's concentrate on the written blurb first.

Simply describe what you think the person with the pen name would be like. What demographic are you appealing to? Let's say that you are writing books for women over 40. Shouldn't you be a woman over 40?

Create a bio that fits in with who the writer of the book claims to be. However, as mentioned earlier, don't give yourself qualifications that you don't have. Use a little bit of poetic license but don't go over the top and pretend to be a doctor or something crazy like that if you're not.

Stick to reality as much as possible and emphasize things that are relevant to your profile without inventing fantastic stories about yourself.

When it comes to putting up a picture, don't use any pictures from the internet that people can find on photo banks. If it's a common picture that people use a lot, someone is bound to spot you as a fake. That's just embarrassing.

Use an AI (artificial intelligence) created picture from https://www.thispersondoesnotexist.com/

Just keep hitting the "return" key on your keyboard until you see a picture that you like for your new author profile. Download it or take a screenshot. No one else has that profile picture and it is now unique to you.

I have to admit, when I first did this, I did feel a bit icky about it. It may come across as a bit deceitful. However, creating a different persona and pen name to write your books is really only keeping with a tradition that goes back hundreds, possibly thousands of years.

You are entitled to privacy and if that means changing a few things to get that privacy, then so be it. Many famous authors have pen names:

Dr Seuss for instance. His real name is **Theodor Seuss Geisel.** Would he have sold as many books under his own name?

And what about Mark Twain? His real name was **Samuel Clemens.**

Everyone knows J.K. Rowling, due to her success with the Harry Potter series. But did you know that she also writes books under the pen name of **Robert Galbraith**?

I rest my case!

Having a pen name is really just a convenient way of writing books. Use one if you want to protect your privacy, or you are thinking of writing in different niches, or maybe you just think it's a more appropriate name than your own.

If you are going to use a pen name, don't use a name that includes a trademark (Amelia Amazon for example). Also, don't use a pen name that is actually a keyword (Barbara Brain Teasers, for example), and don't use the name of a famous author. Amazon may ask you to stand in the naughty corner until you change it.

Try to be original with the pen name and start your brand off with a nice, easy-to-remember name.

Also, to avoid confusion, just check on Amazon.com under books to see if anyone else is using that name. Type the name you want into the search bar and if no other books come up under that name, you are pretty much OK. Stick to your own name if you are writing in one niche and you don't mind people knowing that you write books.

Keep it simple.

Key Points

• Don't overcomplicate using a pen name. Use it for convenience, privacy, or if you intend to write in different niches.

• Create a bio using the personality you feel fits your new author name and the demographic of your readers. Don't use a stock image for your author profile picture, if using a pen name. Use thispersondoesnotexist.com

• Don't feel awkward about using a pen name. Many, many famous authors use pen names. Put it down to poetic license.

• **Poetic License** - the freedom to depart from the facts of a matter or from the conventional rules of language when speaking or writing in order to create an effect.

6
PUBLISHING YOUR BOOK ON KDP

Once you have completed your manuscript and made sure it's properly edited and formatted, you will now want to upload it to KDP. KDP stands for Kindle Direct Publishing and is your book launching platform for Amazon. You will need to have it ready in PDF format for the paperback version and either .doc or ePub for your eBook Kindle version.

Step 1. Save and download your manuscript in PDF or .doc formats to your desktop for your paperback and hardback versions

Step 2 Convert your manuscript doc to ePub format using the free converter https://convertio.co/doc-epub/ and download. This is for your eBook Kindle version

You should now have the PDF & ePub versions on your desktop ready to upload to KDP.

You will also need to upload your book cover to KDP.

You will add your description to your Amazon listing. Create this on a separate document so that you can copy and paste it into KDP.

What is the description?

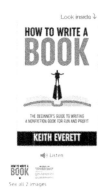

The description is the wording you have on your Amazon listing to describe your book. Use this wisely as people are looking at your description as well as your title and book cover before making a buying decision.

Make sure the opening lines of your description are selling the benefits of the book and are talking about the problem you will solve.

Bold your opening lines to make them stand out.

Describe your book in some detail, telling them how it will benefit them. Give some examples of what the book contains and highlight these by using bullet points.

Add keywords to your description as Amazon's algorithm can pick this up too. Don't go overboard on the description but use as much of the 4000 characters allowed as possible.

Give a call to action at the bottom of the description in bold such as **Scroll up and grab yourself a copy.**

Make your description stand out. It's a good way to entice people to click on the "buy" button.

OK, so we now have our description prepared. It can be entered into KDP either "as it is" or in HTML. (HyperText Markup Language). Now, let's not overcomplicate this.

HTML is an ideal way of creating characters that the basic description box at KDP may not have. You can easily pick up a free Text to HTML converter online.

Here is a free converter if you want to do this:

http://www.unit-conversion.info/texttools/text-to-html/

BUT don't worry if you don't want to add HTML to your description. You can just copy and paste your wording straight into the text box over at KDP.

Right, first things first.

1. Have you opened your free account over at KDP?

YES: Then sign in with your normal Amazon account details

NO: Sign up here: https://kdp.Amazon.com/en_US/

NON-US: Sign up here:

https://kdp.Amazon.com/en_US/help/topic/G202187780

I'm now assuming that you have opened your KDP account and given Amazon your personal details and of course your payment information (this is very important).

Your next step is to go to "Bookshelf". This is where you are going to upload your manuscript and cover, plus add all your book details.

Go here: https://kdp.Amazon.com/en_US/bookshelf

Bookshelf

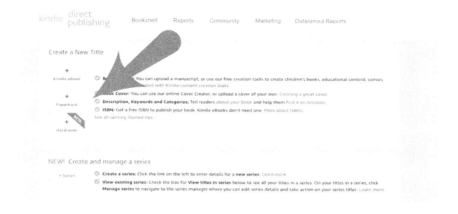

As you can see, the buttons to add your Kindle, Paperback or Hardback books are on the left-hand side.

I would suggest adding your Kindle version first. A lot of the information that you put in there will automatically carry over and populate when you want to add the paperback and hardback versions.

Step 1. Click the + Kindle eBook button

Step 2, fill out the details on page 1.

eBook Details:

Language: If your book is in English, leave it as it is. If not, use the dropdown list to find the language.

Title: Add the title of your book (don't forget your keyword in the title).

Subtitle: Add the subtitle of your book.

Series: Only fill this in if your book is part of a series. If not, leave it blank.

Edition Number: Only fill this out if you are creating a new version of an old book, an updated version. If not, leave it blank.

Author: Add your first and last name if you are the author. If you are using a pen name, add that.

Contributor: For contributors. For example, multiple authors, add them here if you are using contributors. If not, leave it blank.

Description: Here is where you add that lovely description that you've created. If you have HTML code, hit "source". If not, just copy and paste your text into it.

Publishing rights: This is multiple choice. You either own the copyright or the book is in the public domain. You will select the first choice as you own the copyright (more on copyright later in the book).

Keywords: This is where we get a little bit sneaky. You have spaces for 7 keywords here. The thing is, Amazon doesn't actually tell you that they provide 7 boxes for keywords, not boxes for 7 keywords. Most people actually assume you can only add 7 keywords.

In fact, we can actually add more. Use a combination of short-tail and long-tail keywords (remember the lesson in chapter 2 about long-tail and short-tail), and use a comma to separate them, adding a couple of keywords per space.

You should be able to get as many as 12-14 different keywords in here. Make sure that you only use keywords relevant to your book and only use each keyword once.

Categories: you can select 2 categories here. What KDP doesn't tell you here is that you can select up to 8 more later. I'll show you how to do that later in the book.

Age & Grade Range: Don't bother with this unless you are writing books for children, or books considered to be Adult only material.

Pre-order: This defaults to "I am ready to release my book now". If you want to put it on pre-order, check the other option. KDP explains what pre-order is via the link.

Don't forget to click "Save And Continue".

OK, that is the first page taken care of. Congratulations! Take a deep breath, grab a cup of coffee or tea and let's tackle the 2nd page of the 3 pages.

Page 2. eBook Content

This is the page where we are going to upload our Kindle manuscript and cover.

The first thing you will see here is a note on Digital Rights Management. Click on the link for a full explanation, then, either leave it as it is ("no") or click "yes".

Next, upload your manuscript in either .doc or ePub format and allow this time to populate.

Below this, you will be able to upload your eBook cover. Make sure this is in jpg format. Once you upload it, give it time to populate.

Below this, you will find a preview viewer. Click on this and you will be able to approve it if everything looks OK. This does take a little while and even Amazon recommends you go grab a coffee while it is being prepared.

Kindle eBook ISBN At the bottom of the page you will see a section on ISBNs, which stands for International Standard Book Number. A Kindle eBook does **NOT** need one, so leave this blank. However, do click the link for an explanation about ISBNs.

When both your cover and manuscript have populated and you are happy with what you see in the previewer, click "Save and Continue".

Page 3. Kindle eBook Pricing

Commonly known as the "Show me the money" page.

Just kidding.

This is definitely my favorite page.

At the top, you will see a section on enrolling your book in the Kindle Select program. This is where readers who join the Kindle Unlimited program can download your book and read it. You will be paid a small fee per page read.

If you are going to be using KDP Amazon as your primary platform to publish and sell your eBooks, I would suggest you enroll in this program. After all, it's basically free money.

SIDENOTE: Once enrolled, you are tied into using Amazon KDP as your sole distributor for your eBooks for 90 days. You can opt out after the 90 day period or automatically enroll for the next 90 days.

Territories: This defaults to All Territories, worldwide Rights. Keep this as it is unless you only have a specific territory that your book is licensed for.

Primary Marketplace: Amazon.com is the biggest and by far the most profitable so I would keep it on its default setting.

Pricing Royalty & Distribution: Select 70% for your royalty plan.

The difference here between a Kindle or a Paperback & Hardback book is that there are no printing costs for a Kindle. The Kindle is delivered in a file directly to the customer, who can then view it either on a kindle reader or a Kindle online app. KDP does however have a small download charge for each book sold depending on it's file size.

How to price your books

The first thing I would say here is what prices are your competitors charging? I try to keep my book prices competitive based on that information. Having said that, once I have several reviews on the book, I tend to edge my prices up a bit.

Remember: You can come back to this page anytime in "bookshelf" and raise or reduce your prices.

KDP offers different Royalty rates depending on the price of your eBook. If you go under $2.99 or over $9.99, they will only pay you 35%. If your book is priced between $2.99 and $9.99 (recommended) they will pay you a 70% royalty. I tend to keep most of my eBooks between $2.99 and $4.99.

There are exceptions - book bundles, for instance. I'll talk more about this later in the book. But for now, let's keep it simple.

You could start the eBook off at $2.99 and make it £2.99 for the UK and EUR 2.99 for European countries. This is just a suggestion.

Once you have typed in your book prices into the spaces on the left, your actual royalty rates will appear in the far-right column.

Book Lending: If you have enrolled your eBook in KDP select, this will already be ticked.

All you need to do now is hit that bright yellow button at the bottom right of the page that says "Publish Your Kindle eBook".

BOOM!

That's it.

You'll get an email within 24 to 72 hours telling you that it is available for sale in the Kindle store.

Congratulations.

OK, it sounds like it's time for another coffee before we go through how to publish your Paperback.

Publishing Your Paperback

After you have published your Kindle book, a box will appear on the screen asking you if you want to publish your paperback. Click the button and let's get started.

Page 1. Paperback Details

As we have just published our Kindle eBook, all the information has been carried over to this page. We don't have to add anything here.

Just click the button at the bottom of the page that says "Save and Continue".

Page 2. Paperback Content

On this page you can see straight away we have some differences from the page 2 Kindle page.

At the top, you are given a choice to get KDP's free ISBN. As we will be mainly selling our books on Amazon, accept their free ISBN. If you have your own ISBN (you can purchase these online) then you can add that here.

There is a link there, top right, that says "what is an ISBN" click if you want further information at this stage. Personally, I would just accept their FREE ISBN.

Publication Date: Leave this blank if you are publishing for the first time.

Print Options: This is where you are going to get some choices as to the size of your book, the paper and whether you want Matte or Glossy for your cover.

All of this is a personal choice of course and largely depends on what kind of book you are publishing.

If you have illustrations in the book, I suggest you print them in black & white as color printing is more expensive. The cost of printing is deducted before your royalty is calculated, so only use color illustrations if it is absolutely necessary.

Ink & Paper Type: Most non-fiction books are black & white interiors with white paper. You can also choose cream paper. I've never used this option, and it's normally used more for fiction books.

Size: A typical "self-help" or "how-to book" would be 5x8 or 6x9 in dimension. Obviously, you will have taken this into account when creating the manuscript and book cover.

Larger books, like coloring books and puzzle books, are typically 8.5 x 11. The size of your book depends on how many illustrations you have and what size they are. Take a look at your competitor's books. Amongst the book details on Amazon, you will be able to see the size of the book. This book is 6 x 9 in its paperback version.

I've created it as a 6 x 9 instead of a 5 x 8 because of the pictures within the book, a 5 x 8 will make the pictures appear a lot smaller.

Bleed Settings: You will be selecting " No Bleed" for most books. However, there is a link to give you a short explanation of what this means. Bleed settings are more suitable for colouring books, anything that is printed close to the edges.

Paperback Cover Finish: Matte or Glossy. This is a personal choice and it depends on your book. I have experimented with both and for me, Glossy comes out slightly on top visually.

Next, we have the Manuscript & Book cover. Your manuscript will be a PDF, although KDP does allow a .doc file. Your book cover will also be a PDF file.

Upload both files and allow time for them to be processed.

Amazon automatically prints the ISBN & Barcode to your cover.

(If you wish to include the ISBN on your copyright page, which is standard practice, you will need to add it to the manuscript and then re-upload it once your book has been published and you know the ISBN.)

NOTE: If you don't have a cover prepared, there is an option to use KDP's cover creator. Personally, I don't recommend creating your own covers unless you are a graphic designer. We will talk a bit more about covers later in the book.

Book Preview: Launch the previewer and make sure your book and cover look OK. At this stage, Amazon will tell you if there are any faults.

If everything is OK, click "Save and Continue".

If everything is NOT Ok, refer to their link Learn more about formatting and print quality on KDP. I will also be pointing you to various resources later on in this book on how to fix your cover if it is an issue. I don't recommend you using an outside source to fix your manuscript as this means passing your entire unpublished book over to a third party.

Please do not do this.

KDP will tell you what's wrong with your manuscript, if anything.

Page 3. Paperback Rights

Territories: Choose worldwide rights unless your book is only licensed for a specific location.

Primary Marketplace: Choose Amazon.com.

Fill the rest of this page out pretty much how you filled out the pricing page for KDP. You will need to allow for print costs when deciding on the price to charge for your paperbacks.

Also, you will want a 60% Royalty rate (40% is for expanded distribution). Expanded distribution means: Large book distributors can make your title available to other online retailers, libraries, universities, and booksellers (beyond Amazon). Enrolment is subject to eligibility requirements.

Personally, I set all my books to 60% Royalty and I don't touch expanded distribution. Again, this is a personal choice.

Prices. Bear in mind that you want to make a profit here. You get 60% of the selling price, less the cost of printing. Check on your competition to see what price they are charging. Look at how many pages they have in their books, etc., and base your price on that to begin with.

Once you have plenty of reviews on your book, you can begin to charge a bit more.

I start a lot of my 30,000-word books off at $10.89 and bump them up to $14.99 when I have a good amount of reviews (10-20) on them. Bear in mind, if you are going to use Amazon ads, your book costs will rise as you will be paying for advertising costs too to get a sale.

Once you have filled in your paperback prices for each country, you are good to go.

Click the yellow button at the bottom of the page and "Publish Your Paperback Book".

This will take approximately 24hrs - 72hrs. Paperbacks tend to take longer than Kindle books to get approved. It's worth the wait though, seeing your shiny new paperback appear on Amazon for the first time is awesome.

If you wish, you can order up to 5 Proof copies of your paperback or hardcover book before it goes through the Amazon quality review. You can check for any formatting issues or errors before you make your book available for sale. These come with a gray watermark across the front cover saying, "Not For Resale".

Once your book is published, you will be able to order up to 999 Author copies at printing cost.

We have now gone through the entire process of uploading and publishing your Kindle and Paperback book.

You can also publish a Hardback version on KDP. It is the exact same process as for the Paperback, except for two different variations.

1. The cost to publish a Hardback is a little bit higher, so you will need to charge more.

2. The book sizes, therefore the cover sizes are different on KDP. A 5 x 8 becomes a 5.5 x 8.5, etc. You cannot use the same cover that you used for your paperback book. You will need to get that cover adjusted for hardback.

There is a simple solution for this. Go on to fiverr.com and type in "Fix rejected cover". You will be able to get your paperback cover converted to a KDP hardback cover for around $10.

Key Points

• Your manuscript can be in .doc or PDF format for uploading as a paperback or hardback. For Kindle, upload it in the ePub format.

• Your actual book cover should be in jpeg format for Kindle and PDF format for a Paperback.

• If you are uploading to KDP to do a hardback version, your manuscript and book cover will be in the same format as for a paperback but DO REMEMBER the cover sizes are different for KDP hardbacks. A 5 x 8 cover becomes a 5.5 x 8.5, etc. You will also need to get your existing paperback cover adjusted to be a hardback cover.

• Enroll your KDP book in the Kindle select program if you want to lend it and get paid per page read. You do this for 90 days at a time but you cannot sell your eBook anywhere else while it is enrolled in the Kindle Select program.

7
FINDING THE RIGHT CATEGORIES FOR YOUR BOOK

Although you can only add two categories per book when you are in the process of uploading your manuscript, you can actually add up to eight more categories once the book is published.

A lot of people don't know this.

Every time I publish a book, I make it a habit of finding eight more categories to add, both for the Kindle and the paperback versions, as their categories are a little different.

Step 1. How to add up to eight more categories

This is a fairly simple process and KDP even gives you a template to add your book to more categories.

First of all, we are going to go to "contact us", which is situated right down the bottom of the "bookshelf page". Go directly here:

https://kdp.Amazon.com/en_US/contact-us

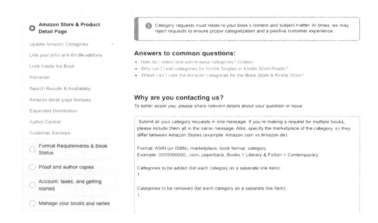

Click on "Amazon Store and Product Detail Page" then select "Update Amazon Categories"

This is the email template KDP wants you to use. You add your book name, type (Kindle or Paperback), and the ASIN or ISBN. Your ASIN number can be found on your Amazon listing under "Product Details".

Add your new categories and number them 1 to 8.

Send the email and Amazon will add your book to the new categories. You will need to do this twice, once for your Kindle book and once for your paperback book.

Step 2. How to find more categories to add your book to

There is a very effective method to do this. You can actually spy on your competitors and use their categories. Use the experience of successful authors.

Why should you do this?

Good question.

You do this because you choose your competitor's books that are obviously doing well, so you can piggyback off their category choices.

How do you know if they are doing well?

One way is to see how well they are doing is to see how low their #BSR (Best Sellers Rank) number is. Go to their book's product page and look for this under "Product Details. You then grab their ASIN number and copy it.

Now go to a free online tool called BKLNK

https://www.bklnk.com/categories_2022.php

This will take you to a search box where we can put our competitor's ASIN number in. Their ASIN is found on their "Product Description" This will tell you which Kindle and book categories your competitor is using.

From here you can copy and paste the categories they are using into your KDP category email template. If they don't have the full eight categories, use what they have and go to your next best competitor's book and do the same until you get the full 8 Kindle and 8 paperback categories. Obviously, check which categories you have already used before submitting them to KDP.

Always make sure you are choosing categories relevant to your book. KDP will not allow you to add your book to irrelevant categories.

Key Points

• You can add your book to a further eight categories for Kindle and paperback once you have published it.

- You can find more categories to add your books to by piggy-backing off your competitor's books.

- Use a free tool called BKLNK to find out which categories your competitors are using.

8
BOOK COVERS - DO IT YOURSELF OR PAY SOMEONE ELSE?

The phrase, "Never judge a book by its cover" may well apply to many situations in life. However, when it comes to publishing books, people most definitely DO judge a book by its cover.

People tend to be very visual beings and what looks good, looks interesting. When your potential customer goes on to Amazon, they are a buyer who is waiting to buy. Rarely do people go on to Amazon to just have "a bit of a browse".

Why should they buy your book as opposed to buying your competitor's book?

Let's look at how "they", your potential customers, look at it. They are buying a book to solve a problem. They have an itch that needs scratching. You need to attract that person to your book.

You do this by having the right keywords in your title that the potential buyer types in.

You have created a wonderful description on your listing, with keywords, that explains what the book is about, BUT most of all, you have an "eye-popping" book cover that says, "BUY ME, BUY ME".

Good book covers sell books. There is no doubt about that, just as bad book covers will put people off buying. Sometimes, you get an author that writes a killer book, but adds an awful cover to it, thus putting people off from actually buying it. This is such a shame.

When you see a tacky cheap-looking cover, you expect the book contents to be cheap and tacky too. If it looks amateurish or messy on the outside, you will assume it's the same on the inside.

Should you create your own cover or should you leave it to a professional?

This is a personal choice. Obviously, when you are starting out on your publishing journey, you do have to consider how much you have to spend on the production of the book.

A good cover can cost a fair bit ($200+). However, you do have to consider the cost of not having a good cover. Sometimes, this can be the difference between selling hardly any books to actually selling a lot.

How do I know this?

My worst-selling book had a fairly cheap cover that I purchased on Fiverr.com for around $25. It was my second book. The book had sold a few copies initially, then stopped selling altogether.

I'm not saying that you can't get a good book cover created on Fiverr; there are some excellent designers on there. However, I didn't do enough due diligence for this book. I replaced it with a $200 cover many months later after I first published it and it did start selling again.

What about doing it yourself?

I would personally only recommend that you create your own cover if you have graphic design skills. You don't want to create an excellent book, only to stop it selling by adding a "pig's ear" awful book cover.

Your book cover is your visual advertisement for the book. How that cover looks to the naked eye will determine how many books you sell.

Think long-term. When a book first goes up for sale on KDP, you may only sell a few copies, or you may sell none at all. Over time, if people like the look of that book and it gets plenty of good reviews, it may start to accelerate in sales and end up selling hundreds, if not thousands, of copies.

Is it worth risking those future sales by putting a cheap-looking cover on it? A good cover will pay you back a hundredfold in the future.

If you absolutely must do it yourself, Canva.com is an ideal place to create a book cover. There is a free and a paid version. Plus, there are plenty of tutorials on Canva. You will find a lot of templates for books there with quite a big free image library. It's a good idea to play around with the different fonts and layouts until you get the hang of it.

You can download a book cover template from KDP in your preferred dimensions, and then upload this onto Canva as a new book cover. After that, build up your book cover design in accordance with the KDP template specifications.

For a paid book cover, my best recommendation is to use 99designs.com This is where you can submit your ideas for a book cover and many designers will compete for your work. This will give you a great idea about which designers you want to use for this and possibly your future books. It will cost you approximately $320.

However, when you have used 99 designs once and paid them, there is no reason why you cannot contact the designer who did your book cover privately and negotiate a price on future work. I generally pay around $200 for a complete set of book covers. This consists of Kindle, Paperback, Hardback, and Audible, plus some mockups of the book to use for posting on social media, etc.

Key points

• Always judge your book by its cover.

• Always pay for a decent cover if your budget allows. The better the cover, the more books it is likely to sell.

- Only attempt to create your own book cover if you have graphic design skills, or your budget is extremely low. 99 designs is a good place to go for a great cover. You can also get a decent cover done on Fiverr.com but do your due diligence.

9
GETTING REVIEWS

I think at this stage of your self-publishing journey, it is so important to stress the importance of getting reviews for your book. This is not an either-or situation. Without reviews, your book will go to the Amazon graveyard and die. And no one wants that to happen.

Why publish a great book and just leave it to the marketplace to decide whether it wants it or not?

As a new book, Amazon's algorithm will show your book a little bit more than usual in the first 30 days as it's still new, and in this 30 day period, Amazon will decide on its worthiness to its audience.

The algorithm looks for movement on your book. It looks for views, sales, and reviews. Therefore, it is your job to get as many eyeballs on your book as quickly as possible.

This chapter is all about getting reviews so I will kick off with my most promising strategy.

1. A Facebook Group

As I covered earlier, a lot of people don't like Facebook. I want you to forget all about that. You are in business to sell books, lots of them.

Forget about making friends (although it's nice if you do). Facebook is a means for you to create buyers for your books. There are a million authors out there, many probably selling books similar to yours, and you want to stand out. You need to put any "I hate Facebook" ideas on the back burner for now and welcome this powerful Social Media platform into your life.

Facebook has 2.91 billion members as recorded in the last quarter of 2021. That's 1 in 3 of all people on Earth.

Many of those people read books. Some of these people could be reading your books.

Let's buckle down and look at a strategy on Facebook that actually works.

Step 1. Create a Facebook group in your niche.

If you already have a Facebook account, create a group by clicking here:

https://www.facebook.com/groups/feed/

In the left-hand column, you will see a link that says **+create new group**. Click that and create your group. Add a cover picture to the header.

Start to add some content to your group. This could be pictures, relevant blog posts, etc., etc.

Then, start adding your Facebook friends to the group. If you don't have any Facebook friends yet, join some groups in your niche and start adding some of the members of those groups. Don't overdo this though as Facebook penalizes you if you try to gain too many friends too quickly per day.

Request around 50/75 people a day to join your group. Do this slowly, this should take around 20-30 minutes per day. Within a short period of time, depending on how attractive your niche is, you shouldn't have any problem getting your first hundred people in your group in the first couple of weeks.

Bear in mind: most people will ignore your requests to join your group and when they do join it, most people won't review your book. Facts are facts. Many people operate on a "what's in it for me" basis and with reviews, we cannot incentivize people to do a review for us.

What we can do for people is to create great content in the group and actively engage with as many people as possible.

Amazon wants unbiased reviews from people who have read your book. This is understandable. You have to ask people nicely, give them a copy of the book and then send them some nice reminders afterward asking them to give you an honest review.

Keep following up.

This is how you do this:

Don't give your book to friends and family to review. Amazon keeps track of your contacts who are connected to you through Amazon, and can tell if you both have the same address or if you have sent them a gift in the past using Amazon.

Let people review your book who have no direct connection to you. Having Facebook friends review my books has never been a problem for me. However, stay within the Amazon rules on reviewing.

You can check out Amazon's review rules here:

https://keitheverett.co.uk/reviewrules

Before you start asking members to review your book, let's look at how you can get people in the group on your side.

1. Post good compelling content in the group daily

2. Welcome members to the group

3. When you form the group on Facebook, you have the option to create a list of questions for new members to fill out. Make those questions count.

Questions

A) Ask them to agree to do an occasional book review for you. This pre-warns and warms them up when you ask for a review in the future.

B) Tell them you encourage interaction, but will not tolerate any spam in the group.

C) Ask them to join your email list (more on this later in the book).

Ask your Facebook group members to review your book.

This is pretty simple, but it is also time-consuming. Most members of your group will be on Facebook messenger. Make sure that you are also on messenger.

Initially you will be inviting friends into your Facebook group, however, some people will join organically. Invite those people to be your friend on Facebook if they are not already, and simply message each one telling them that you have a new book coming out soon and ask if they would like a free copy (digital) in exchange for a review.

Some will ghost you, some will say no, and some will say yes. When I got my first 100 members in my group, around 30 offered to do a review. When I actually published my book, I found that around 20-25 people would still be agreeable to doing one.

Here's how you give your book to reviewers:

1. **Set your Kindle book price to Zero on Amazon.** You do this in your "bookshelf" by using the dropdown list to the right of your Kindle book where it says "promote and advertise".

Look for "Run a Price Promotion" - "Free Book Promotion". You will have to set this one or two days in advance of using it and you get a maximum of 5 days to promote it for free.

Once your book is available for free, you then send your would-be reviewers the link to your Kindle book page and tell them to download the book as soon as possible as it is free only for a limited time.

Your potential reviewers will then download the book to either their Kindle reader if they have one or more likely, they will just download it to their Amazon account where they will be able to view it on a free Kindle viewer.

*** Ask your reviewers to always download from the link***

Why?

There are two kinds of reviews. Verified and unverified. If you give a person a PDF digital copy and ask them to leave a review, it will be "unverified".

If you ask them to download it directly from your Amazon listing, it becomes "verified, even if you give it away free. This is very important as it's only "verified" reviews that cross-pollinate across to all Amazon platforms. In other words, let's say that you ask someone using the Spanish Amazon platform at Amazon.es to leave you a review.

If you just send that person a PDF copy of your book, the review will only stay on Amazon.es and it won't be a verified review. Whereas, if you ask them to download it, it becomes "verified" and their review will eventually end up on many of the other Amazon sites too.

Once your Facebook reviewers have the link to your book, give them 7-10 days to review it. Follow up with a message saying something like "What did you think of the book? I'd love to hear your thoughts."

Some of those people will ghost you, some will say they haven't finished the book yet. Some will say they forgot, and some will say, "Yes, it was good," or something like that. To those people who have finished the book but have not yet left a review, give them the direct link to where they can leave their review.

The link will only work if you add the ASIN of the book you want reviewing on the end.

This link is: https://www.amazon.com/gp/product-review/ (put your ASIN here)

Keep following up with people and keep building your review team. The more active members you have the better, as some will drop out over time. Always thank each reviewer personally after they've left a review.

Treat every reviewer as a personal friend. Many of mine have become personal friends, If you can, do them a favor, however never review their book if they are an author - review swaps are against Amazon's terms of service.

Let all reviewers know that they are a valued ally (they are). Like and comment on their Facebook content, leave comments on their blog or videos if they have them.

I give every member who reviews my books a mention in the Facebook group itself. It lets everyone in the group know that we are a review team, and we value them.

Another good idea is to leave snippets from your book/s as a post in yourFacebook group. This helps community spirit as you are giving people snapshots of your book for free, and you may end up encouraging more reviewers when you do this, or even people who may go ahead and buy it.

Whenever I am publishing a book in the group, I always add a picture of the book in a post telling people that the book is coming. When people review the book, I take a screenshot of the review and place it in the comments underneath that post, linking it to the reviewer.

You can never run out of ideas to post in the group. I joined a paid blog subscription service called medium.com for $5 a month. This gives me lots of content to post each day. I also post YouTube videos in the group about things related to my niche. Keep your Facebook group happy and they will stay with you for a long time.

Continue to grow your group by constantly inviting new members, increasing your friend's list, and posting daily. Also, keep adding people to your reviewer group.

Eventually, you are almost guaranteeing a certain amount of reviews on each book.

So, even if you HATE Facebook, get to love it. It will get you many reviewers, and as you know, reviews are vital to a self-publisher.

Other ways to get reviewers.

2. Create an email list.

Another fairly simple way to get reviews is to ask your email list. You may not have an email list at this early stage yet. However, as an author, you really do need to create an email list as early as possible.

Why?

You are in the business of creating fans. Fans become buyers and readers of your book, so having an email list of potential customers to email each time you produce a book is extremely useful.

How do I create an email list?

First, you need to purchase an autoresponder. What this does is it puts everyone who signs up to your list at the beginning of any email sequence that you create.

You can either send your subscribers a sequence of pre-written emails every 3 days or so, or you can send a broadcast to your list. A broadcast is a one-off message.

Which autoresponder company you use is up to you, there are good and bad ones out there. I personally use Getresponse, I have found them to be very reliable and I've used them for years in a previous online business.

Getresponse also has very easy-to-create capture pages for you to design and get people to sign up to your list. In order to get people to sign up in the first place, you do need to offer an incentive. I would suggest creating a short report with some tips in it relating to the niche you are in.

For example: If you have just published a book on the Top 100 Ideas To Lose Weight, perhaps you can create a short report with 10 ideas in it to give away as an incentive for them to sign up. Obviously you put links in this free report to your book on Amazon.

I personally give away a digital copy of one of my earlier books. Check it out here: https://keith.subscribemenow.com/ .That page was created in Getresponse.

What do we do next?

Once you have set up your offer, your capture page, and your email sequence, you are ready to go. Whoever you choose to use for your autoresponder, they will always have plenty of tutorials on how to do this. So, don't worry if you feel this is a little bit too technical. I promise you, with a bit of practice, you will be fine.

Now, you are all set up. You can advertise your offer and capture page link in the front and back of your book. You can advertise it in your Facebook group or personal Facebook page. You can also use Twitter, Pinterest, or even YouTube if you create videos.

Once you get some people on your email list and you have a book coming out, ask your list, "Who would like a free copy of my latest book?, all I ask is an honest review on Amazon in return". Just ask them to reply to the email and BOOM! You now have them on your review team.

3. Pay to give your book away for FREE

It's OK, I haven't gone stark raving mad. This really does work. Freebooksy has over a half-million subscribers in total, 165,000 to 175,000 of which are non-fiction readers. They will send as many people as possible to your free book. Each person goes to your book's link on Amazon and downloads the book.

https://www.freebooksy.com/for-the-authors/

Although you are giving your book away for free, any reviews you get will automatically be verified as people have to download the book from Amazon. Freebooksy is not a review site — it's a site to get your book in front of readers. You may only get a small percentage of people actually giving a review, or of course, none at all.

Remember earlier when I showed you how to set your book for free? Well, you first want to find out what spots are available with Freebooksy. Then set your book for free in advance to the specified day that you have booked with Freebooksy.

They then email your book details to their huge list for a one off mailing. The last time I did this I got around 1500 downloads on Amazon and a few reviews. Expect your non-fiction book to cost between $65 & $75 to advertise on Freebooksy.

https://www.freebooksy.com/freebooksy-feature-pricing-4/

Let's look at the benefits to you.

You will be getting lots of free downloads of your book, and this will get your book into a lot of people's hands. The benefits of that are fourfold:

1. You are showing Amazon that your book is popular, even though you are giving it for free. Your #BSR will probably start to reduce on Amazon, exposing your book to more people.

2. If you've been shrewd enough to include your opt-in link to your email list in your eBook, you are probably going to get several people opting into that list if your offer is enticing enough.

3. Some of the people downloading your book will probably give you a review if you ask for it in your book.

4. Some of those people MAY even buy the paperback version of that book if they really liked it.

Sure, it's $65 or $75, but you do have to speculate to accumulate. This is a good way to launch your book — at least you will start to see some movement on it. There is nothing worse than a book that just sits there all day and doesn't do anything.

4. Do a Review Video

I love this idea as it not only gets you reviews, it can also get you sales. I simply review my book on video. I do a short three to five minute video and I go through the main points of my book. I upload my video to YouTube and include good keywords in the title and the description underneath.

I then encourage people to click the link under the video to buy it on Amazon, OR if they would like a free copy in exchange for an honest review, I tell them to email me, and I then invite them into my Facebook group and (of course) the review team.

NOTE: If you are using a pen name, review the book on behalf of the Author with the Pen name.

There are many ways to get reviews out there, and certainly too many to list here. I would suggest that you try all four that I have listed above. These are the only ones I use at present and they seem to work fairly well.

There are lots of sites out there where you can give your eBook away for free. If you do decide to try any of those, make sure that they all link back to Amazon.

You want to get as many eager eyeballs on your book as possible. The more people you get downloading and buying your book, the more reviews you'll get.

It does take time. I tend to use Amazon Ads to give my books a bit of a "shove" but I only start using advertising once I've got around 15 reviews on a book. Social proof is very important in the buying process — no one really likes to be the first person to buy a book. By seeing plenty of reviews on your book, it puts the potential customer's mind at rest that this choice of book could be a good one for them.

I hope you really CRUSH it with reviews. Good luck.

Key Points

• Get busy on Facebook. Facebook groups are free to create and they are great places to find book reviewers.

• Be careful who you give your book to for review. Friends and family are not a good idea as Amazon may see the link between you and them, and view the review as biased.

• Never incentivize a review. And never pay someone for a review, this goes against Amazon's terms and conditions and could get your account shut down.

- Email lists are a great way to keep in touch with customers and potential customers. Plus, they are a great way to get reviews.

- Give your book away for free on Freebooksy. YES, you have to pay for the privilege, but it can be well worth it.

10
HOW TO SELL MORE BOOKS

One of the more obvious ways to sell more books is to use Amazon ads. Amazon ads are a strange beast and can certainly help you to get more eyeballs on your books.

1. Amazon Ads

It would take a whole book to explain the intricacies of Amazon ads properly but you can get a more detailed explanation here: https://advertising.Amazon.com/

Here is the shortened version: Amazon ads work on a pay-per-click or pay-per-view basis. You can let Amazon find the right keywords for your book (auto) or you can add your own keywords (manual).

You can choose the price you want to pay for clicks or views and Amazon will show your book to potential customers. People who bid more will get a better chance to get their book in front of a potential customer for the keyword, as you are bidding against other people.

I tend to use Amazon ads when I publish a new book, but only when it has around 15 reviews on it. Otherwise, you are sending people to a "cold book", a book that people haven't yet shown any interest in.

Amazon ads can be very profitable, however, it will probably take a while for your campaigns to show a profit as a lot of the keywords you choose may not turn out to be a good fit for your book. It really is trial and error and it could mean losing money in the interim period.

2. Your Website or Blog

Apart from just leaving your book as it is on Amazon, This is by far one of the cheapest ways to acquire customers. Blogging can be a great way to get your content seen.

My blog: https://keitheverett.co.uk is updated regularly and shows content in my niche, which is personal development, self-help, and how-to books.

A blog can be put together quite cheaply and easily. You only need a domain, some hosting, and a free blog from Wordpress.org.

Or, you can get someone on Fiverr.com to put a nice blog together for you and add a few graphics for under $100.

I share my blog content on Facebook and other social media channels such as LinkedIn, Twitter, and Pinterest. This produces eyeballs on my content. I link some of my posts to my books on Amazon and I also have small 300 x 250px ads appearing down the side of the posts.

I don't use flashing banner ads or any of that 1990's crap

I use a free tracking link WordPress plugin called "pretty links" so I can keep track of who is clicking on what. This tells me which links are most popular and how many people are clicking on them.

3. Podcasts

This works well whether you are doing the podcast yourself or you are a guest. Depending on your niche, there is probably a podcast out there to suit. I've appeared on a few myself and the best one was David Walker's "Internet Marketing Revealed"

People really do pay attention to podcasts and there is always an opportunity to sneak the name of your book in there somewhere.

There are plenty of videos on YouTube on how to start a podcast. A podcast really is a little bit like a talking blog in which you will be airing episodes and possibly interviewing guests. You can end up with a large following and you can then monetize that following by talking about your books.

This does work and, if done properly, can bring you in a nice flow of extra sales over time.

4. Review Videos We spoke about these in the previous chapter, they are great for getting reviews but also as a wonderful tool for getting sales. YouTube, Instagram, Facebook & TikTok spring to mind.

5. Simply Ask

If you want to sell your book, sometimes you have to be bold. Go into niche-related Facebook groups and ask the admin if you can post a book review video. Many will say no, but some will say yes. You can even contact blog owners and ask them if they will do a book review of your book. .

Asking is simple, get used to it. You will be asking for reviews and if you can ask for reviews, then you can ask people to feature your book review video. If they say no, ask them if you can offer a free digital copy of your book to people in the group to get reviews. This may well get you some reviews and possibly even some sales of the paperback version.

Some blog and Facebook group owners are only too glad to have someone outside of themselves providing a little bit of content.

You could also offer to do a guest post on their blog.

The list is endless.

People are always looking for content for their blogs and Facebook groups. Keep asking — every 'no' is a step nearer to a 'yes'.

Other social media platforms

If you like using **Instagram**, this is a great platform for promoting your book. A lot of authors don't realize that Instagram has countless marketing opportunities for books.

Don't forget that it has **over 500 million active users** and is currently rated the #1 social media engagement tool for brands. It can help you to generate compelling content, position your brand (your book), and connect you to a wider audience. There are many self-published authors whose social media presence is almost solely limited to Instagram and they are enjoying great success.

The 5 basics for using Instagram

1. Create a strong author bio and speak to your target reader.
2. Add a link to your book on Amazon, your author website and/or blog.
3. Just like Facebook, you have to engage with your followers. Like other people's content, follow them, and comment on their posts.
4. Make regular posts and keep your content fresh and interesting. Don't just keep posting pictures of your book cover, but try to share content that relates to your niche. Instagrammers are greedy for new images, so keep posting content they will like. Share pics about your upcoming launch or new books. You can use the free version of Canva to create some stunning visuals for your Instagram account.
5. Use hashtags and descriptions for each image or video you post to Instagram. These really help with optimization and will get like-minded users to find your content. You only need to use about 3-5 relevant hashtags and the most popular hashtags you should include are #instabooks and #bookstagram.

To get followers on Instagram, you have to start following other users. This is easy to do. You can search for specific hashtags in the search bar and follow any accounts that seem to fit your target audience. Hopefully, they will follow you back. You can also follow people that they follow, and so on.

You only need to spend about 30 minutes per day doing this and will soon see your following grow. These are all potential buyers for your book.

Networking with other writers or bloggers who review books is a good way to increase reviews and attract a wider audience. Follow bloggers and engage with them. You can even ask them to review your book for you.

Avoid offers from uninvited people wanting to review your book for a fee. These are not worth the money and can even be scams.

Although I haven't used it myself, **TikTok** seems to be becoming more and more popular with self-published authors. It's worth checking it out if you feel up to the challenge and aren't camera shy!

The app has nearly 100 million monthly active users in the United States alone, and a massive community of readers using the hashtag BookTok. It's worth noting that it's mostly popular with the under 30s age group so you need to consider if your book niche fits that demographic. Otherwise, it's probably not worth it.

It's a lot easier to reach people on TikTok than on other social media platforms because you don't need a single follower. You just have to upload a video, which might be seen by thousands of people. You can talk about your book, read some quotes from it, talk about what inspired you to write it, share tips from your book, or anything you think will get views.

DON'T use TikTok as a "sell, sell, sell" platform. You won't be successful, TikTok users value creativity, humor and authenticity so connect with them on those levels and don't over-promote. If people feel like they have an authentic connection with you and like your videos, they might buy your book.

Key Points

- There are plenty of places that would welcome you either talking about your book or sharing some content that leads to your book.

- Amazon ads can help you sell your book. They may look a little bit tricky at first and there is a learning curve but it can be mastered if you persevere.
- A Website or a blog is a good place for selling books. Keep your content regular and interesting in order to attract visitors. Monetize your posts and the blog or website itself using ads.
- Podcasts can get your face and your book out there. Many podcasts would welcome someone talking about their book.
- Do your own book review videos on YouTube. Share them on social media and in Facebook groups (get permission first from the admin).
- Instagram is a great platform to use if you want to promote your book to a wider audience. You can also network with bloggers who might be prepared to do a book review for you.
- TikTok is worth a shot if you enjoy making fun videos that will appeal to a younger audience.

11
USING AMAZON MARKETING TOOLS

Your goal is to sell as many books as possible. It's also in Amazon's best interest to increase your sales, which is why they give you some help in promoting your book on KDP.

Amazon A+ Content

One tool you can use is Amazon's **A+ Content** for paperback and Kindle eBooks. It's a powerful book-marketing feature that anyone who self-publishes can use on their product page.

You can enjoy the benefits of advanced formatting and rich media content to enhance the customer's shopping experience and persuade them to buy your product. You can use it no matter what genre your book is, or which niche.

To make the most of this tool, all you need is some basic marketing savvy and some nice images. You can check out your competitor pages to see how they are using it to their advantage and although it might seem unnecessary, my philosophy is, if other people are doing it, it must be worth it.

Here are some of the perks:

- Amazon KDP A+ Content is free to use.
- You don't need to have registered your book on KDP Select to take advantage of it.
- You can publish A+ content in multiple languages.
- Your new content will appear within eight business days.

Below is an example of some A+ content that appears on one of my my book's Amazon pages.

CREATING A+ Content

Before you dive in head first, think about what images you want to use, what images you already have or might need to create, and what written content you should add.

To use A+ Content, follow these steps:

Log into your KDP account and select 'Marketing' from the top toolbar. Once opened, scroll down until you see the option for A+ content. Select the Marketplace you are interested in and then select Manage A+ Content.

You can enter your ASIN or just get started.

You will see all the module layouts. These include a variety of options, such as text-only, image-only, image left and text right, and so on. You'll also see different graphic size requirements and text options.

Decide which layout will show off your nook to its best advantage for your book.

Now start to add your content and images. You can save it as a draft and finish it at a later time if you like.

Apply ASINs. You can find the ASIN on your product detail page. You cannot add an ASIN from anywhere else.

Next, review your content and submit it! As long as there are no obvious problems, such as images being too big, your content will be reviewed by KDP and appear on your page within eight business days.

There are some rules to follow if you want to use A+ Content and you will receive an automatic error message if you try to submit content that doesn't meet the requirements.

The main things to watch out for and not fall foul of Amazon's rules are:

1. Image file requirements
2. Text formatting requirements
3. Requirements about mentioning book awards, etc.
4. Use of trademarks
5. References to other books and unverified claims

6. Use of customer reviews
7. Mention of pricing, promotions, or discounts
8. Phrases like 'latest product', 'The best on the market', and so on
9. References to Kindle Unlimited

You will see 12 module examples on the amazon online guide, but the builder tool in KDP has 17, so there are plenty of options.

Here is the direct link to the guidelines: https://kdp.amazon.com/en_US/help/topic/G4WB7VPPEAREHAAD

Using Author Central

When you get into self-publishing, you are building a brand, just like you would in any other business. On the **Amazon Author Central** page, you can do just that. It's a homepage for you to set up an account as an author (even if you are using a pen name) and you can create a profile page, including your book titles, and any other information.

Why do you need it?

- It provides a central hub for readers to learn more about you and to educate them about your books.
- You can manage all your book details when it comes to listings on the Amazon page.
- It's a free personalized page on a powerful, global platform (Amazon.com) to showcase your products.
- You can build out and customize your author page to generate interest in your books from your customers.
- It helps you to build your brand.

As soon as you launch your first book, you can set up your profile. You could say that an Amazon Central account is a great substitute for a website if you don't have one yet. It can generate interest in your books, attract more readers, and increase your visibility on KDP. It also helps you to build a web presence.

To join Amazon Author Central once you have published a book,

1. Go to **Amazon Author Central** and click "Join Now."
2. Sign in with your regular Amazon.com username and password.
3. Read the Terms and Conditions then click "Accept."
4. Enter the author name your books are published under. Select your books from the ones that appear to set up the account.
5. If you can't see your book on the list, search for it by title or **ISBN**.

Note: Your book must be available for purchase on Amazon in order to set up an Author Central Amazon Account.

1. Amazon will send you a confirmation email to finish creating the account.
2. Once you have the go-ahead from Amazon, you can begin to optimize your Author page. This is an ongoing project and you can refine it whenever you launch a new book or blog post.

Here are some ideas to turn it into a professional-looking page:

1. Add an Author photo
2. Add your Author Bio
3. Add your books
4. Add some book reviews
5. Add editorial reviews (US only)
6. Add Video book trailers for your books
7. Add the Direct feed to your most recent blog articles (US only)
8. Remind people to click the + Follow button and follow you

You want to build customer loyalty when you aim to publish several books for your Amazon self-publishing business and this free space lets you do that so use it! I know quite a few self-published authors who just plonk their book, or books, on the KDP bookshelf and don't curate any content to attract customers who land on their page.

Follow these tips:

Create a good bio. Take the time to write a nice bio that anyone browsing your page can connect to and get them buying your books. Even if you are using a pen name, you can write something that will be of interest without having to make wild claims. Say why you are an expert on the subject(s) in your book(s) and any fun facts.

Connect your blog feed (US only). If you have a blog, you can connect it to your readers here. Each time you post a new blog, it will feature on Amazon Central.

Only available if you are in the US at the moment, you can use this feature by signing in to your Amazon Author Page>Blogs>Add blog>enter RSS address> select Add.

Customize your Amazon URL. Instead of a long, complicated link, customize your Amazon URL so it looks professional. Your Amazon URL directs people to your Author Central Page when you share it on social media, blogs, in email signatures, etc., where they can check out your books and learn more about you as an author.

To do this, go to the Author Central Profile tab and click on 'add link' next to Author Page URL. you can use the suggested URL that appears or edit it to suit yourself. If the URL you input is available, click Save. It will take about 30 minutes to go live.

Add promotional videos. Although Amazon doesn't let authors post book trailers on the product pages, you can post one on your author page. If a customer clicks on your author profile from your product page, your author video will show up on your author page. It might be a trailer for your book or a welcome video and you can add up to 8 at a time. Videos are great marketing tools to use although they must meet the Amazon specifications:

1. Be either mov, mpg, avi, flv, or wmv format
2. Be smaller than 500MB
3. Be less than ten minutes long

To add your video to your Amazon Author Central Page, sign in to your Amazon Author Central account. On the Author Central Profile tab, click Add video>Browse>Select your video file>Click the box to confirm you own or have rights to the video>Upload video.

It can take up to 24 hours to process and you should receive an email from Amazon when the video is ready. Go to the video, review, then approve it.

Claim your books. Not many self-publishing people know this, but when you publish a new book, the first thing you should do is go to Author Central and claim that book as yours. This links your title to your Amazon Author page.

To do so, go to **Amazon Author Central,** click on Books>Add more books>search using either author name, book title, or ISBN>click on 'This is my book'. Your book will appear in your lineup within 24 hours and you can begin to review the sales ranking and Amazon customer reviews.

Add editorial reviews (US only). Reviews sell books. That's why you want to take full advantage of reviews left by your readers. You can also add snippets of up to 5 reviews in the editorial section. To do this, go to your Amazon Author Page, select the Books tab, choose the book you want to add reviews to, select Add under Editorial Reviews and follow the instructions. Preview the review and Save when ready.

Create a Book Series Page. If you've published a series of books in your name (or pen name) you can showcase them here. You are making it easier for customers to buy all of the books in one purchase and gain insights into how many books a reader has purchased from your series too. To create a series page, go to the Bookshelf in your KDP account, click on Create series, enter the details and click on Submit updates.

Make sure to update your Amazon Author Central regularly to keep it current and attractive. As soon as you have some good reviews on your books, make sure to include them in the editorial reviews for the book page. Update your author bio every 12-24 months, adding anything interesting that will give customers something to read about. Keep blogging so your content can be refreshed every now and again.

Pre-Orders

There's nothing better than generating a buzz about your upcoming book and now Amazon lets you do this for eBooks. It takes some planning but it is a great way to promote a new book using Amazon's KDP Pre-order features.

If you are on your first book, the idea of promoting it before it's even up for sale can sound a bit daunting. You don't need to spend a lot of money on this but can start pushing it on your social media feed and blog posts. It works really well if you already have a book on KDP and have a mailing list because it can be difficult to drive traffic to a pre-order if you are a newbie.

Even though Amazon gives you up to 90 days for pre-orders, that's far too long. Since you aren't going to be spending a ton of money on promoting it, you don't want to wait months on end. I'd say a few weeks to a month, tops and it's important to choose a date that you know you will be ready by as well.

Promote your new book on email blasts to start driving interest, as well as on your Facebook posts, blog posts, etc. Price it at a special pre-order discount to entice buyers. You can always raise the price later.

When setting up your eBook, select a date in the future for when you want it to be available. A detail page will be generated for the eBook and customers can make their orders anytime leading up to the release date. It will also be delivered to them on that date.

After you set up a pre-order, a timer will appear to help you keep track of your deadline. You have until this deadline to make any changes to your book, but I recommend that you upload your files at least ten days before the release date, or even sooner. That way, if there's a quality issue, you'll have time to fix it and resubmit it.

You also need to know that:

- Your book goes live at midnight local time on your selected date
- You will be informed of pre-orders immediately

- You will get sales reports from the day it goes live
- Royalty payments will follow the normal schedule

If your cover isn't ready, you can even use a dummy one as a placeholder for now and add the final one when ready before the launch date. While pre-orders can be useful, bear in mind that most readers prefer to buy a book once it has been published and not before.

Join the Amazon Associate Program

The Amazon Associate program is a good way to earn extra income on your book. Anyone can sign up and receive a commission when they refer someone to Amazon who ends up buying a product.

When you register with the Amazon Associates Program, you can add a special link to all your book promotion links and posts. This can generate money for you online from the Amazon KDP affiliate program fees and commission sales. Although commission on an eBook might not be a lot, the bonus is that you can earn a commission on **any other items** that people buy on the Amazon store after being directed there through your link for a 24 hour period.

There are many different ways you can use the Amazon KDP affiliate program on your blog or website. But let's look first at how you can get started.

To get started,

To get started, go to the Associates home page and register.

https://affiliate-program.amazon.com/

Click on the Join Now For Free button.

Choose the program for the country you are in.

Once you are registered, set up your Amazon Stripe. It will appear at the top of your screen every time you log in and visit an Amazon page.

Now you can copy Amazon's associate product links from your site stripe to your books. You can use them on social media, on your blog posts, or even your website.

Note:

1. Do not use your own Associates account to shop for your own purchases. If you do, you run the risk of being kicked out of the program. Remember to log out of Associates before you shop for yourself.
2. You can go to Your Earnings summary and then click Reports to see the number of clicks your book has received.

Amazon is always tweaking its services so you may find that one day you can do this or that, and the next day discover that something has changed. That's why you need to keep up with what is going on there.

Nevertheless, it is a really good platform to help you promote and market your business so take advantage of it as much as you can.

Key points

- Amazon has a lot of free marketing tools to help authors promote books.
- Curate an engaging product page using A+ Content.
- Use Author Central to help your customer learn more about you and your products.
- Pre-orders are a way to create a buzz about an upcoming book you aim to publish.
- Consider joining the Amazon Associate Program to earn extra income from your book.

12
AUDIBLE - TURNING SOUNDS INTO PROFIT

Up until now, we have concentrated on books. We could have three different ways to sell our book: the Kindle eBook, the Paperback, and the Hardback. Now, let's look at a fourth way.

Audible for audiobooks.

Imagine, if each time you self-publish a book, you have 4 different formats. With 10 books published, you will have 40 separate products out there, all hopefully making you money.

Audiobooks

A lot of people actually prefer to listen to a book than read it.

Reading a book is not always convenient and sometimes, just listening can be more enjoyable for a person, especially if their preferred way of learning is auditory.

Our aim here is to transfer our book manuscript into an audiobook. You can do this by first creating an account at ACX. https://www.acx.com/. Add all your details and don't forget to add your banking details too. You want to get paid, right?

ACX is the production platform for Audible. As you probably know, Audible is owned by Amazon. When you publish an audiobook on ACX, your book will appear on both the US & UK versions of Audible, plus all worldwide platforms of Amazon and even Apple iTunes too.

To create your audiobook you are going to need a producer (narrator). ACX has thousands of narrators on their platform who can narrate your book, with prices ranging from around $50-$250 per finished hour.

To be honest, although I don't suggest always looking for the cheapest, sometimes the $250 an hour narrators are really no better than the $50 or $100 an hour narrators.

It's all a matter of choice of course, and when you open an account at ACX, you will get to listen to as many narrators as you want before deciding on the one you like.

You could, of course, narrate your own audiobook to save money. I would not recommend you do this unless you have a pristine radio voice and you have the best equipment to record on.

If this is not the case, I would invest in a narrator from ACX.

The first step.

Here is a guide from ACX that explains the basics:

Please note: If you are listening to this book on Audible, all clickable links and pictures are in the accompanying free PDF.

https://www.acx.com/help/print-publishers/200484620

You can't publish an audiobook on ACX until you have first published your Kindle eBook. Once you have opened an account at ACX and you have published your Kindle book on Amazon, you now search for your book using the ACX search.

On the front page of acx.com you should see this:

In the top right-hand corner click on "add your title".

This will take you to the ACX search.

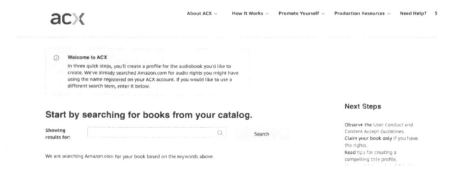

You can search by the title of your book. However, it seems to work much better if you search by your ASIN number.

Once you've added your book, ACX will ask you a series of questions in order to get your book listed on ACX.

Unfortunately, I can only show this if I am actually adding a title myself at the time of giving you those instructions.

However, ACX makes it fairly simple and straightforward.

You will need to know how many words your book has. You will also need to have a short script prepared for the narrator to read. I usually take two or three paragraphs from the introduction of my book and copy and paste them into a .doc to upload.

Most of the information on your Kindle book will be transferred automatically across to ACX. You don't need to upload your Audible book cover yet. You will do that once you approve your narrator's work.

From here on in, you will simply be choosing a narrator. That might mean auditioning several narrators until you find the one who suits your book. You will set a price that you are prepared to pay and then you will make an agreement with ACX and the narrator.

You will be offered a choice of making your audiobook exclusive to Audible (recommended) or making it available to Audible and any other platforms of your choice. For exclusive rights, Audible will pay you a 40% royalty. For non exclusive rights, the royalty is 25%.

Also, you will be given a choice on how you want to pay your narrator: by per finished hour (PFH), or by a 50/50% royalty split (if they agree).

Personally, I would go for the per finished hour option as you could be giving a lot of money away in a 50/50 split if your audiobook takes off and does well. Again, it's a personal decision and depends on your budget.

When you pay per finished hour, you are only paying for the length of your book NOT how long the producer takes to complete your book.

What you have to think about when choosing a narrator.

You need to choose a narrator that you feel fits the style of your book. Narrators come in all different styles and types of voices. You can request to have auditions only from male or female narrators, US accents, British accents, etc. Choose whatever style you think will give the end-user the best experience of your audiobook.

When listening to an audition, ask yourself if you could listen to three hours or more of this narrator's voice. If the answer is a resounding NO, then don't hire them.

I have audiobooks aimed at the male and female market, therefore I have a male and female narrator to narrate them.

I think when people buy a book from a male author, they tend to expect a male narrator, and vice versa, although it's not written in stone.

I like to have a narrator that is easy to work with. Obviously, you won't find this out until you start working with them but you can get a rough idea at the start by seeing how quickly they answer your emails, etc., and how professionally they answer your questions. I like to choose a narrator that has a positive voice and one that has done several projects in the past.

You can easily find out all this information on ACX. You have access to as many narrators as you wish to choose from and you are not rushed into making any decisions.

When you are ready to go ahead, your narrator may take three or more weeks to create the entire book's recording. You do have an opportunity, in the beginning, to get a 15-minute sample of your book recorded by your narrator. Once you approve that, the narrator will go to work to record your book. You will have already uploaded the full manuscript to ACX for the narrator to read.

Some narrators produce the recordings one chapter at a time. This gives you a chance to OK them or request any changes. Other narrators record the whole book, then upload all the files to ACX for you to listen to and approve.

Most of the time it will all go smoothly, Ive worked with three narrators on ACX up until now and they have all been very easy to work with.

Once you approve all the files, you will sign off the work, pay the narrator, upload your audiobook cover and then send everything off to be approved by ACX. This can take eight working days, sometimes more, sometimes less. It depends on how busy they are.

Once your audiobook is published, you will need to do a few things.

1. Send a copy of your PDF manuscript via email to **support@acx.com.** ACX will then add this to your customer's library when they purchase your audiobook. ACX will also add a message to your audio-

book description telling the potential customer that they will get a free PDF. This is not obligatory but it may help the sale of your audiobook.

2. Once your audiobook is published, you will be given 25 US and 25 UK codes to give out to reviewers. You will be able to give these out to your friends and family so that they can download your book for free. Ask them to listen to the entire book and then give you an honest review on Audible.

Please note: Audible has a different policy when it comes to reviews compared to Amazon. Whereas reviews from friends and family are not allowed on Amazon, Audible seems to be OK with this. This of course can change at any time.

Audible has two platforms: audible.com & audible.co.uk , both of which are free to join. Someone living in the USA can leave a review on the UK site, and vice versa.

Audible also has a paid subscription service (for customers). There are various offers on there to join, but the standard subscription is $14.95 per month, for which a customer gets a credit for one title per month within that membership. This varies between the US and UK versions of audible and in some cases can come with a 1-month free trial.

The reason I mention this is because this is very important when it comes to deciding the length of our audiobooks. Let me explain.

A 30,000-word book produces approximately 3hrs of recorded audio. The way that Audible sets the price of an audiobook is by the recorded length. For instance, a book that is 2hrs and 59 minutes long goes on sale for much less than a book that is 3hrs long.

3hrs, or 30,000 words is the "sweet spot" when it comes to the length of an audiobook.

I create all my books over the 30,000-word mark where possible, which gives us a nice retail price of at least $17.94. If you go under the 3hr mark, the retail price drops rapidly and personally, I've not found it very cost-effective to create audiobooks of 1 - 2 hrs in duration.

I'm not saying you can't make money producing short audiobooks, I'm just saying it probably won't be that profitable. Of course, you can produce MORE short low content books and then bundle them together in future to make 2 in 1 or even 3 in 1 audiobooks. These are called:

Bundles.

Obviously, we can only do this once we have produced 2 or more books in the same genre.

This is a way that you can make even more profit using the same books. It took me a while to do this as there is a fair bit of messing around producing a 2, 3, or 4 book bundle. But it can be very profitable.

You start off by combining the manuscripts of 2 or more books into one book. So, book A is your first book, followed by book B, etc. You have one table of contents but you clearly separate each book.

Your table of contents would read:

Book 1. Chapter 1. Chapter 2. Etc.

Book 2. Chapter 1. Chapter 2. Etc.

Once you have combined the manuscripts, you now need to get a new cover made for your bundle. This new cover should show it as a 2 in 1 book. Amazon frowns at the word "bundle" and may not allow that word on the cover or title.

Choose the wording "2 in 1 book" or "2 in 1 value pack" etc.

Also, for Amazon, on the front cover of your book, don't show any images that suggest the customer will be receiving several hard copies of books in the mail. If you must show multiple books on the cover, show them as "flat" images.

Upload your 2 in 1 (etc.) book to Amazon and publish it as a Kindle, and also a paperback if you choose.

You then go through the same process of finding your ASIN number on Amazon, and adding it to the ACX search (as shown previously).

The difference here is that you don't require a narrator to do any recording, except for a couple (or more) new intros & outros for the bundle.

First locate the files for the books that you want to bundle. You will find these in the "projects" tab in the menu on your ACX page.

You then need to download the files carefully from each book and put them in a separate folder on your desktop. Once you have downloaded all the files to you desktop, you will need to re-upload them one at a time to your new book listing, starting with book 1.

You also need to create a space for a new file in front of each book's introduction. This is for your narrator to record a brand new introduction.

Remember, this is a new book, therefore you will need a new introduction in front of every book you are including and one new outro at the end.

You will now contact your previous narrator via email to ask them to record the new introductions (and outro). Narrators usually charge around $10 (or £10) per recorded intro and outro. I've only created one 2-book bundle so far and my narrator charged me £30 for all 3 new pieces of narration.

Once you have put this all together, you pay your narrator privately in this case, you add your new cover, and send it off to ACX for approval, you now have a nice new 2 in 1 bundle book for sale.

All it costs you is a little bit of time and effort, a new cover, and a small charge from your narrator. Bundles can be very profitable as Audible members want to get the biggest bang for their buck (their free audiobook each month) and often choose longer and more expensive books.

Please note: A book may only appear in any bundle once. If you have 5 books, A, B, C, D, E,

Your first bundle is A, B, C

Your second bundle must be D & E, you can't include any of books A, B, or C again in a bundle.

Key Points

• In order to publish on Audible, you must have created the book and published it as a Kindle ebook first.

• Find your book a lot easier in the ACX search bar by typing in your book's ASIN number.

• Your royalties on audiobook sales are 40% for selling exclusively with Audible and 25% for non-exclusive rights.

• You can pay your narrator per finished hour or as a 50/50% royalty split if your budget is low. However, I would recommend paying per finished hour.

• The longer your audiobook is, the higher price it sells for. It is recommended that you create a book over 3hrs long (30,000 words+).

• You can bundle books together to make even more profit.

13
SETTING YOUR PRICE AND GETTING PAID

I mentioned pricing earlier on and wanted to talk a little bit more about it and how royalties work on KDP. After all, a business is all about making money and you need to know what to expect.

There are two main aspects to the costs involved in selling eBooks and paperbacks/hardbacks on KDP:

1. The sale cost - what KDP will charge you for each book sold.
2. The sales commission KDP takes for selling your book.

We already know that your royalty rate for eBooks is 70% of the retail price if you have the ebook on sale for anything from $2.99 to $9.99. If you price your book between $0.01 and $2.98 or greater than $9.99, you get paid 35% royalties. That's why it's best to self-publish your eBooks between $2.99 and $9.99 to receive a higher share of royalties.

NOTE: Amazon will only pay 35% royalties in certain countries unless the author enrols it in the KDP Select Program.

Kindle eBooks

Amazon also charges for delivery of eBooks priced at the 70% royalty rate option, depending on the country it's being delivered to. This is in addition to the sales commission you pay KDP for each sale.

KDP charges $0.15 per megabyte (MB), which is the file size of your eBook. For every book you sell priced between $2.99 and $9.99 at the 70% royalty option, there is a minimum charge of $0.01. There is no delivery charge for books priced below $2.99 or above $9.99, with the 35% royalty option.

What royalties will you get?

Let's say you price your eBook at $2.99 on Amazon.com and the file size is 1 MB and is being purchased by a US customer on the Amazon.com website.

The royalty payment formula Amazon uses is:

Royalty Rate x (Retail Price − Delivery Costs) = Royalty Earned

So, we can make this calculation:

70% x ($2.99 − $0.15) = $1.988

Your royalty earned for each book should be $1.99, or just under $2.

What you need to remember is that the "file size after conversion" is much smaller than the file you uploaded because KDP processes the eBook file for delivery, and the final file size is smaller. So, the most reliable way to calculate the Kindle delivery fee for your eBook is to go to KDP's pricing page after you have uploaded the file and see what the tool says.

The only way to avoid this charge is to price your eBook at the 35% royalty option. This isn't the best option for most of us, but you might want to consider it if you are publishing books with a lot of images, such as cookery books or art books.

Sales commissions and your royalties

You will need to pay KDP a sales commission for their services, which is based on your royalty rate:

- For 35% royalty: the Amazon sales commission is 65% for books priced below $2.99 and above $9.99
- For 70% royalty: the Amazon sales commission is 30% for books priced between $2.99 and $9.99

The royalties KDP takes are still much lower than what a traditional publishing house would be taking if you published through them. This is what makes self-publishing so attractive to many people. You are basically cutting out the middleman (i.e. the publishing house) and selling directly to the store owner (i.e. Amazon KDP).

What about VAT?

More than 160 countries around the world charge VAT (value added tax) on purchases, excluding the United States.. Amazon adjusts your royalty to include VAT, regardless of the royalty rate. The calculation is:

- 35% royalty rate x (list price − applicable VAT) = royalty
- 70% royalty rate x (list price − applicable VAT − delivery costs) = royalty

Not all eBooks are eligible for a 70% royalty so you might want to take that into consideration when deciding how to price your book.

1. Some territories/countries are excluded, although most English-speaking countries pay the higher royalty. You can find more information here. https://kdp.amazon.com/en_US/help/topic/G200634500
2. For eBook sales in Brazil, Japan, Mexico, and India, the royalty is 35% unless you join KDP Select.
3. If you also have a paperback or hardback edition, the list price of your eBook must be at least 20% below the price of this to qualify for the 70% royalty.

Why Amazon might offer your book for a lower price

You might receive less than you expect if you put your eBook on sale on another eBook platform like Barnes & Noble for a lower price. In this case, Amazon will automatically match that price. This is because, when you sell your book on Amazon, you are agreeing not to sell it at a lower price anywhere else.

If this happens and the price falls below the minimum 70% list price requirement, you will receive the lower 35% royalty.

What royalties do you get in a KDP Select Countdown Deal?

When you sign up for KDP Select, you can run a reduced-price sale for a one-to seven-day period. When you do this, you retain the 70% royalty if the sale price is lower than $2.99. Here's an example.

Your book is listed for $4.99.

You get 70% of $4.99, minus delivery costs and any taxes.

If you run a Countdown Deal to sell the book for $1.99, you receive the same 70% royalty (less delivery charges and taxes).

You can reduce your eBook price whenever you like, but you won't get the 70% royalty if the price is below $2.99. The only way to keep the higher royalty is through a Countdown Deal.

You can learn more about Countdown Deals here: https://kdp.amazon.com/en_US/help/topic/G201293780

What about eBook aggregators?

If you want, you can pay for services like Draft2Digital, Smashwords, Bookbaby, and IngramSpark, which are all eBook aggregators. They distribute your book to more than one online retailer (e.g. Amazon, Apple, Barnes & Noble). These companies charge you a fee or keep a percentage of the book sales for managing your eBooks. Since most eBooks are still sold in the Kindle store though, you need to consider if it is really worth using an aggregator or not.

KDP Print books (paperback and hardcover)

When it comes to print book pricing for KDP Print, things are a bit more straightforward. The key cost here is what it takes to manufacture your book and how that is affected by things like:

- Which country your book is being sold in
- How many pages your book has
- Your printing choices (e.g. premium color, standard color, black and white)

The good news is there are three factors that don't impact cost:

1. The book dimensions. Whether it is 8.5 x 11 or 6 x 9, the manufacturing cost is the same.
2. The paper color (cream or white). Only color printing matters.
3. The cover finish (glossy or matte).

To calculate your KDP Print printing costs:

1. Upload your files to KDP Print.
2. The calculator that appears will show you a cost.
3. Use Amazon's pricing tables.
4. Use Amazon's Printing Cost & Royalty Calculator.

Trim size, bleed settings, and cover finish do not affect the cost of printing. You also need to note that not all paperback book dimensions can be printed in hardcover format.

Paperback sales commission and your royalties

Now that you know the cost for manufacturing your printed book, you can calculate the sales commission. Your royalty is 60% of your list price minus printing costs.

- **(list price x 60%) – printing costs = royalty**

Of course, it's impossible to sell a print book for less than it costs to print it. Amazon calculates the number for you like this:

Printing cost / 60% (royalty rate) = minimum list price. You cannot charge more than $250 or 250EUR for your print book.

If you want to sell your book on your website, bear in mind that you can't price it higher than what it is on sale for in KDP. It should be the same price as your Amazon listing. Equally, if you try to sell it for a lower price anywhere else, Amazon will match that price and reduce your royalties.

What about expanded distribution royalties?

Amazon can make your book available to other online retailers like Ingram (the parent company of IngramSpark) and this is called **expanded distribution**. Books eligible for this receive a 40% royalty, basically because Ingram needs to be compensated for making your book available to retailers, such as Barnes & Noble. This applies only to print books, and not eBooks.

Why Amazon might offer your book for a lower price

A lot of people new to self-publishing ask why Amazon reduces the price of their book and the answer is that it's trying to meet or beat competitor pricing. Your royalty doesn't change though, in line with Amazon's terms and conditions.

Download your Amazon royalty report

Amazon provides you with detailed royalty reports for all sales during the previous month on the 15th of each month. On June 15, 2022, for example, you will receive a royalty report for May 2022.

The report outlines how many sales you have made for each book at both the 70% and 35% royalty rate, as well as any books borrowed from the Kindle Unlimited and downloaded for free from a KDP Select Free Promotion.

You can download your reports by going to https://kdp.amazon.com/reports and then clicking "Prior Months' Royalties."

You can also check your sales dashboard Amazon for live sales reporting but these sales do not include detailed royalty calculations.

You can also check out your sales history, information about payments, pre-orders, promotions, and Ad Campaigns.

When will I get my Amazon royalties?

That's the question we all want to know.

Royalties are paid out every month, approximately 60 days after the end of the month in which the sale was reported (90 days for Expanded Distribution sales) as long as you meet the minimum threshold for payment.

Once you have successfully set up your payment options on your KDP account, you can choose from the following payment options:

Direct deposits

Direct deposit payments can take 1–5 business days to show on your bank account from the payment date.

Wire transfers

Wire payments can take 5–10 days.

By Check

Check delivery time frames vary depending on location. It can take up to 30 days for the check to reach the address in your KDP account.

If you are being paid by a wire transfer or check, your payments must have accrued a minimum amount of earned royalties through your book sales. If you don't meet the minimum amount, a running total will be kept and you will receive the payment once you meet the requirements.

Amazon pays you 60 days after the end of each month's sales.

For example, if you earn $2,000 in royalties from book sales in May, Amazon will send your royalty payments 60 days after the end of that month's sales. You will therefore receive royalty payments for your May sales on August 1.

Patience does pay off, eventually!

Key points

- Familiarize yourself with the fees Amazon charge for both ebooks and hard copies.
- Learn how to calculate your royalties.
- Keep up with your sales by downloading the Amazon monthly royalties report.
- Decide which payment option works best for you.

14
A WORD ABOUT COPYRIGHT

Once you have made your book public, you will want to ensure that its contents don't get stolen and used by someone else to cash in on your hard work. Unfortunately, this happens quite frequently and is known as copyright theft. This means that someone, somewhere, is basically stealing your book and selling it under another name.

You might think that you own the copyright to the book once it is written, and you would be correct in thinking that. But that doesn't stop someone from downloading your ebook, then uploading it as their own with a different cover. It's also possible that a bookstore buys one copy of your paperback, makes thousands of copies, then sells them to customers. In this situation, they are profiting off your book while you receive nothing.

If that happens, the onus is on you to prove that the book actually belongs to you, which might take time, money, and loss of earnings. Audible is beginning to ask for proof of copyright from users when submitting files after reports of audio files being stolen so it's something to think about.

To avoid your intellectual property, i.e. your book, from being copied, the best thing to do is purchase a Copyright Certificate, which will prove that it belongs to you. After that, it can only be copied with your permission and anyone doing so behind your back is legally liable.

Depending on where you are, you can obtain a Copyright Certificate online or by post. In the UK, there is no official body holding copyright records. Your work is protected by right, as in most EU countries, by the Berne Convention. Having said that, it's still going to be a painful experience to have to go through legal proceedings to prove your case if you get caught up in a nasty copyright war.

The best bet is to buy a Copyright Certificate, which can be obtained on a number of legal websites offering the service for around £29.99 to £39.99.

If you live in the US, head to the US Copyright Office's landing page at copyright.gov/registrations. Fill in the relevant details and submit your application at a cost of $65 for one book. If you live in the UK or another country and are planning to market your book in the US, you can apply for a copyright certificate on the above link.

It's important to remember that when you publish a book through KDP, you aren't handing over your copyright claim. You're simply licensing them to publish and issue your work. You can unpublish your book at any time as it always belongs to you.

Creating a copyright page in your book

As you will have noticed, all books have a copyright page at the beginning right after the title page. This should include some essential information such as:

1. The copyright notice. This has the little © symbol that you might have seen being used like this: ©2022 Keith Everett
2. The year of book publication
3. The author's name or pen name
4. Reservation of rights
5. Copyright notice
6. Book editions

7. ISBN Number
8. Disclaimer

Do I need a disclaimer?

It's worth adding a disclaimer as it protects you from any possible libel actions. For example, if you are writing in the health and wellness niche, you don't want someone chasing after you accusing you of causing them harm.

It's unlikely that you would face this kind of problem, but it's always best to stay on the safe side. General disclaimers look something like this:

The advice and strategies found within this book may not be suitable for every situation. This work is sold with the understanding that the author cannot be held responsible for the results accrued from the advice in this book.

You can also make your rights reserved more specific with something like this:

No part of this book may be reproduced or used in any manner without the prior written permission of the copyright owner, except for the use of brief quotations in a book review.

In other words, let the readers know that they are reading your book and applying your advice at their own risk. You can find many examples of disclaimers available to download for free if you do a Google search.

Other information you can include

For eBooks, you can add a section explaining your rights. It won't protect you from piracy but it makes your rights clear. It can look something like this:

This ebook is licensed for your personal enjoyment only. This ebook may not be re-sold or given away to other people. If you would like to share this book with another person, please purchase an additional copy for each person you share it with. Thank you for respecting the hard work of this author. No part of this publication may be reproduced, distributed, or transmitted in any form or by any means, including photocopying, recording, or other electronic or mechanical methods, without the prior written permission of the publisher, except in the case of brief quotations embodied in critical reviews and certain other non-commercial uses permitted by copyright law.

If you have an ISBN or different ISBNs for different versions of your book, you can add this information to your page if you like. You could also add the Amazon ASIN, but it really isn't necessary. If your book is an updated version or new edition, you can mention that in one line, saying something like *Revised Edition 2022*

You might also want to add credits. These could include things such as *Cover Design by Joe Bloggs, Edited by Sam Smith, Layout by Sarah Smith, and so on.*

It's not obligatory to include a copyright page in your book, but it doesn't take two minutes to do if you want one. Apart from protecting your work from thieves, it also adds to your credibility.

Protect your work and enjoy the rewards!

15
THE BIG SELL-OFF

Let's assume that you have now been trading for four or five years. Your publishing company is averaging around $8k per month in profit.

This is not an unreasonable amount for a publishing company that has been around for this long. You probably have many books, perhaps thirty or forty, of which around eight or so are doing very well (20%).

Those eight books between them bring in the bulk of the profits, while the other 32 books are selling the odd book now and again.

This is not a made-up scenario. The publishing group to which I belong has many people who are in this situation. There are also many more people doing even better and of course, several who are not doing a lot.

This is like any other business: some people will do exceptionally well, while others will fail or not do very much. It really depends on your determination, drive, and how badly you want success.

For some, self-publishing is a hobby, which is fine. But for others, it can be life-changing. So, when you reach a time when your business has been showing consistent profits and your publishing company has been running for a few short years, it can be a very attractive proposition for a buyer.

You might want to sell it and take the money.

You can sell your publishing business, lock, stock, and barrel to one of the many people out there online who are looking for a business just like yours.

Note: when I say you are selling the business, you are actually selling the assets, not the company itself.

One of the most popular places to sell a publishing business is on Empire Flippers. https://empireflippers.com/

There are many business people out there with large sums of money sitting in savings accounts that are not earning much interest, or wish to expand existing businesses.

These people are your buyers..

A publishing business can be a very attractive place for someone to "park" their money. People are very interested in a business with a fairly passive income model behind it.

Self-publishing requires little "hands-on" effort once the books have been published.

This makes the valuation much higher than you would think, with some publishing businesses going for 40-50 times their monthly income.

If your publishing business has been netting around $8k per month over a sustained period, your company could now be valued between $320,000 & $400,000 on Empire Flippers.

Of course, you will have fees to pay to Empire Flippers, and there is capital gains tax to pay. However, Empire Flippers do all the hard work. They negotiate with the potential buyer and they transfer all your assets from your business over to the buyer. It's a complete service.

Once sold, you now have a nice large sum of money to do what you like with.

You can always start another publishing company. You will have to use a different name on your books, of course, but anything is possible. One of my colleagues sold his business recently for multiple six figures. He is now enjoying his newly-found fortune and looking forward to starting a brand new self-publishing business.

Anything is possible if you are prepared to work hard in self-publishing. I hope you have enjoyed this book. It gives you a great insight into how to get self-published and how to turn it into a successful business.

Your goal from now on should be to keep producing great books, keep getting better and better at writing, getting plenty of reviews, creating audiobooks, and enjoying the journey.

Key Points

- A publishing business that has made proven profit and has been trading for a few years could be worth 40 to 50 times its monthly profit.
- Once you sell a publishing business, there is nothing stopping you from creating a new one. You will have to change author names though.
- Make it your goal from now on to produce multiple books of quality, get plenty of reviews, create an email list and spend time increasing your assets. This will reflect in the eventual selling price of your business

CONCLUSION

Thousands of new books and eBooks go on sale online every month. It's a highly competitive market, with more and more people getting into self-publishing.

Despite that, there's no reason why you can't make a solid business out of it.

Once you find a good niche and micro-niche, work on producing a great quality product. People want value and they recognize it when they see it. A lot of the self-published books on KDP are really bad quality. Many of them have been rush jobs prepared on the cheap. You will notice this as soon as you see the cover or use the 'Look Inside' feature.

Customers want to feel respected and you will chase them away if your book looks tacky, badly written, and dog-eared. If your page description is lacking in information and you have no author profile, it's hardly reasonable to expect someone to bother to buy your product. There are a lot of truly stunning book covers and content descriptions on KDP so aim to meet that higher standard.

In business, just as in life, once you get a bad reputation, it's very hard to live that down. That's why you need to work hard to please your customers by offering them a pristine product. Not only do you want to sell your book, but you want to encourage them to come back and buy your next book, and the one after that. This is how you build brand loyalty and make money.

If you really want to make a go of it in the self-publishing business, it's no good diving in without knowing how to swim. That's why I wrote this book, to give you all of the information you need to make it happen and be a success.

Do your homework and prepare to:

- Find the niche you want to start off with.
- Find those keywords to grab the customer's attention.
- Create a great manuscript that speaks to your target group.
- Hire a professional ghostwriter to create high-quality book content.
- Choose a catchy pen name or use your real name - it's up to you.
- Get a professional to design an eye-catching book cover.
- Publish your eBook, paperback, and hardback books on the Amazon KDP store.
- Select the right categories for your particular book to be found in.
- Learn all about KDP pricing and royalties.
- Use social media, blogs, and Amazon marketing tools to get your book noticed.
- Turn your book into an audiobook to reach an even wider audience.
- Keep providing fresh, valuable content in your social media groups to retain interest.
- Protect your work with copyright certificates and pages.

Once you have done all of that, don't just sit back on your sofa and wait for the money to start rolling in. There's always something you can do to increase your sales. Keep up with the market trends, learn new digital skills, keep growing your review group, talk to other self-publishing people, and follow those who are successful in the business.

What are they doing right that you can learn from? What can you do to improve your business?

Make changes

If your book isn't selling, you might need to make some changes, such as changing your book cover. It might sound like an expensive job but if you feel that the current one isn't working, it's worth the investment. Ask people you know who buy books, their opinion before you do this and see what response you get. Do they love the present cover, hate it, or are indifferent?

Look at your competitors books to see which ones are selling well, do the covers stand out?

You might need to change your keywords and categories, refining them until you get it just right. This costs nothing and can seriously take you from unsatisfactory sales to more purchases and royalties earned.

Alter your price as well to test the waters. This also costs nothing and you might find that lowering or increasing that can bring you a bigger return. A lot of it is trial and error, so keep working at it to generate sales.

If you feel like your description or author bio could do with an update, do it. It only takes minutes and could make all the difference. You can change your information as often as you like so don't leave it up there to go stale.

Some last thoughts

According to a report by The Association of American Publishers in 2020, **US ebook sales revenue was put at $1.94 billion** in 2019. **Amazon sells 68%** of that revenue!

In the most recent statistics of ebook vs hardcover sales on Amazon from 2016, **Amazon sold $4.6 billion** more in hard copy books than ebooks. While that figure is a bit dated (Amazon isn't keen on sharing their sales statistics) we can assume that more paperback books are still being sold than ebooks.

As for **Audible** (owned by Amazon), it currently ranks as **the most used audiobook app.** Their #1 selling genre is romance, by the way, (and I thought romance was dead!). In the UK alone, audiobook sales have increased by more than 30% since 2020.

In total, Amazon generates about **$386 billion per year**, and around **$5 billion of that comes from book sales.** Amazon is set to maintain its top position as the leading eCommerce website for book buying.

Amazon's **Kindle Direct Publishing** services give them **a massive lead** over other online bookselling websites because it not only stocks them, but produces and sells them too.

There is massive business potential out there for anyone who wants to get into self-publishing and make a profit. The market is huge, demand for books is as popular as ever, and plenty of people will want to buy your book.

It's time for you to do it!

A FINAL NOTE FROM KEITH

When ever you get the urge to give up. Take my advice and DON'T do it. I have over 40 years of experience in business and I don't say this lightly but this is the best business I've ever come across.

When I wrote my first book, I really didn't know what I was doing, I procrastinated and wrote it like I was writing a 30,000 word blog post. It didn't flow very well and ended up being totally re-written.

We learn by doing. It's the only way.

That one book finally got published. It was hard work, but the feeling of getting your first book published and on Amazon is one of euphoria. Self publishing is like a drug, a wonderful drug. Seeing your work in print and selling that work over and over again is a wonderful feeling.

Watching your business grow month on month is so EXCITING!

I hope you take the steps to get your self publishing business up and running and selling books all over the world. I still check my KDP stats for book sales each and every day just like a kid at Christmas.

Go through this book again and again until each step starts to feel more comfortable. But don't forget, on your second reading, do the steps as you read along. Don't be like some authors who spend years before they finish writing and publishing their first book.

Set out a block of time each day and get busy. Money loves speed.

At first it will feel like you are running a marathon up a mountain. It won't always be like this. Your first published book will be a trial and error exercise. After that, it will get easier, I promise you.

I have a little favour to ask you, it will only take 5 minutes.

Make An Author Happy Today!

I hope you found this book helpful. If you did, I would be eternally grateful if you could spend a few minutes writing a review on either Amazon or Audible (depending on where you bought it)

When you post a review, it makes a huge difference in helping more readers find my book.

Your review would seriously make my day

Thanking you in advance

Keith

RESOURCES

Keith's Author Page

https://www.amazon.com/-/e/B0926WKHF5

Other Books written by Keith

How To Write A Book

Awesome Kindle Book Ideas

Money Mind Crush

Millionaire Mind Crush

Other books published by Keith and written by Rebecca Collins

Rebecca's Author Page

https://www.amazon.com/-/e/B0999J1BWF

Keith's Website

https://keitheverett.co.uk

Keith's Facebook Group

https://www.facebook.com/groups/inspiredtomakemoney

Free Gift

https://keith.subscribemenow.com/

Printed in Great Britain
by Amazon

46493161R10076